D0192219

# THINKING SKILLS

# DAILY BRAIN TEASERS

# AGES 7–9

**PIPPA HARRIS-BURLAND & MIKE FLEETHAM**

# CREDITS

**Authors**
Pippa Harris-Burland
& Mike Fleetham

**Illustrations**
Nick Diggory

**Series Designer**
Anna Oliwa

**Editor**
Wendy Tse

**Designer**
Melissa Leeke

**Assistant Editor**
Catherine Gilhooly

Text © Pippa Harris-Burland & Mike Fleetham
© 2006 Scholastic Ltd

Mike would like to thank teacher Jo Bourne for her valuable contribution to some of the ideas in this book. Pippa would also like to thank Henry and Daisy, her children, for their ideas, and a special thank you to David.

Designed using Adobe InDesign

Published by Scholastic Ltd
Villiers House, Clarendon Avenue,
Leamington Spa, Warwickshire CV32 5PR

www.scholastic.co.uk

Printed by Bell and Bain Ltd

456789      789012345

**British Library Cataloguing-in-Publication Data**
A catalogue record for this book is available from the British Library.

ISBN 0-439-96543-8
ISBN 978-0439-96543-9

The rights of Pippa Harris-Burland and Mike Fleetham to be identified as the authors of this work has been asserted by them in accordance with the Copyright, Designs and Patents Act 1988.
Material from the National Curriculum © The Queen's Printer and Controller of HMSO. Reproduced under the terms of HMSO Guidance Note 8.

The publishers wish to thank:
Network Educational Press Limited for the use of 'Action ryhmes for gaining attention' from *The ALPS Approach Resource Book: accelerated learning in primary schools* by Alistair Smith and Nicola Call © 2001, Alistair Smith and Nicola Call (2001, Network Educational Press Limited).

# CONTENTS

# DAILY BRAINTEASERS FOR AGES 7–9

## WHAT IS 'DAILY BRAINTEASERS?'

Daily Brainteasers 7-9 is a collection of over 160 ideas for activities that will develop the five thinking skills highlighted in the National Curriculum.

## HOW IS IT ORGANISED?

Different children prefer different learning styles: visual (seeing), auditory (hearing), tactile (touching); kinaesthetic (movement). The activities have been grouped into four chapters, each focusing on one of the learning styles. Further information can be found at www.newlearningstyles.org.uk

## WHAT DOES EACH BRAINTEASER CONTAIN?

● Each brainteaser details the thinking skill to be developed:

Information processing: collecting, sorting, classifying, sequencing, comparing and contrasting information.

Reasoning: giving reasons for opinions and actions, drawing inferences, making deductions, using precise language to say what they think, making judgements and decisions based on reason/ evidence.

Enquiry: asking relevant questions, posing and defining problems, planning what to do and how to research, predict outcomes and anticipate consequences, testing conclusions and improving ideas.

Creative: generating and extending ideas, suggesting hypotheses, applying imagination, looking for alternative, innovative outcomes.

Evaluation: evaluating information, judging the value of what is read, seen, heard or done, developing criteria for judging the value of their own and others' work or ideas, and developing

confidence in their judgements.

*(adapted from National Curriculum, 2000)*

● Each brainteaser states if there is a link to another learning style.

● It details the subject link – many of the brainteasers are activities that complement objectives in the units from the Year 3 and Year 4 QCA schemes of work.

● Each brainteaser gives suggestions for organisation. Many of the ideas can be adapted for individual situations.

● A list of resources is given and some refer to useful websites (live at the time of publication).

● Instructions for carrying out the brainteasers are given in the WHAT TO DO section. Where possible these have been directed at the children themselves.

● Answers to problems have also been given where appropriate!

## HOW SHOULD THEY BE USED?

To ensure balanced coverage across thinking skill, learning style and subject area, we suggest several approaches. Go with an approach that best meets the needs of your class:

● Develop a daily brainteaser time – start of the day, after break or lunch, at home time

● Choose a brainteaser from each chapter in rotation

● Use subject-specific brainteasers to begin or end a lesson in that subject

● Choose a weekly focus of either a thinking skill or learning style

● Some brainteasers require no preparation and last just a few minutes – others need resources, preparation time and up to 15 minutes' delivery time.

Further ideas are available at www. thinkingclassroom.co.uk where you can also contact Mike and Pippa.

## FREAKY FIREWORKS

**THINKING SKILL:** creative thinking
**SUBJECT LINK:** PHSE
**LEARNING LINK:** auditory
**ORGANISATION:** individuals
**RESOURCES:** firework name generator

| First part | Second part |
|---|---|
| Roman | Volcano |
| Traffic | Lantern |
| Super | Wheel |
| Fire | Rocket |
| Sparky | Burst |
| Glowing | Tree |
| Monster | Shower |
| Green | Shiver |
| Yellow | Fountain |
| Sky | Bang |

### WHAT TO DO
● Show children the firework name generator. Ask them for any additions.
● Ask them to combine any first part with any second part to create a new firework.
● Share firework names. Ask them to add another first part and another second part.
● Share the new names.
● Repeat the process until the new firework has a six-part name, for example, Monster Bang Yellow Shower Fire Rocket.
● Ask the children to draw a picture for their new firework.

*Note: use this as an opportunity to reinforce safe behaviour around fireworks.*

### NOW TRY THIS
**1.** Add a third column to the generator – perhaps animals/noises/colours/sizes and so on.
**2.** Encourage them to make up other types of generator, like a birthday cake generator.
**3.** They could draw their favourite creations.

## OOH LA LA

**THINKING SKILL:** creative thinking, evaluation, enquiry
**SUBJECT LINK:** modern languages
**LEARNING LINK:** kinaesthetic
**ORGANISATION:** pairs
**RESOURCES:** pencils; compass or something circular to trace around; card and paper; scissors; colouring crayons/pencils; labels and pictures of pizza toppings in different languages, for example, cheese, fromage (French), käse (German), queso (Spanish), formaggio (Italian), tomato, tomate (in French, German and Spanish, but pronounced differently), pomodoro (Italian), (do the same for mushroom, peppers, tuna, sweets, ice cream)

### WHAT TO DO
● You are going to make up a new recipe for pizza.
● Firstly, cut a large circle out of the card for your pizza base.
● Stick on as many labels as you like for your toppings.
● Pizza is Italian, and it is called the same thing wherever you go.
● If you draw a piece of cheese and stick it on top, what could you write on it?

### NOW TRY THIS
Working with another partner, compare your pizzas in different ways, such as, *Which one would be best for a small child? Which one would be best for an adult? Which one is simplest? Most complicated? Which one would cost the most? Be cheapest?*

# ODD ONE OUT

**THINKING SKILL:** enquiry
**SUBJECT LINK:** music
**ORGANISATION:** groups of three or four
**RESOURCES:** sets of four photographs (or word labels) of musical instruments, with an odd one out in each set, for example, violin, cello, double bass, harp

## WHAT TO DO

● Split the class into groups of three or four. The children work together to find the odd one out in the sets of photographs – they are all musical instruments.
● Ask them to discuss and identify the odd one out in each set and give reasons for their choice.

## NOW TRY THIS

Try more difficult 'odd one out' games. Compare and contrast other aspects of instruments, such as shape, size, colour, and sound. For example, a harp might be odd one out in the example because it is the biggest instrument.

# TIMELINE

**THINKING SKILL:** reasoning
**SUBJECT LINK:** history
**ORGANISATION:** individual
**RESOURCES:** paper and pencil; timeline template for each child or timeline on the board; pictures of different periods in history relating to children's previous learning; labels with the period names jumbled up on the board, such as Iron Age, Egyptians, Tudors, Romans, Victorians

## WHAT TO DO

● Point to the jumbled pictures and labels on the board. Tell the children that history has been muddled up. You need them to help you unravel it by placing the pictures and labels correctly on a timeline.
● Draw a timeline on the board. Mark off five short lines where each period will be written.

● Ask them to copy the timeline onto a piece of paper.
● Ask, *If the Romans are placed on the third mark, where are the other periods placed?*
● After the children have written the periods of history onto their own timeline, work together to order the pictures and captions on the timeline on the board.

## NOW TRY THIS

Discuss the results and promote 'What if?' questions such as, *If the Romans had not invaded Britain, what might be different now? If the Egyptians had buried their dead kings at sea, what might be different now?*

# WORD PLAY

**THINKING SKILL:** information processing
**SUBJECT LINK:** literacy
**ORGANISATION:** pairs
**RESOURCES:** sticky labels; felt-tipped pens; positive adjectives, for example, *happy*, *funny*, *clever*, written on the board

## WHAT TO DO

● Ask if anyone knows what an adjective is.
● Tell the children you want them to think up some positive alliterative adjectives to go with their names – these must be related to thinking, learning and/or the classroom.
● Write examples on the board, such as Willing William, Enquiring Ella, Friendly Fred and Creative Caroline.
● Split the children into two groups. Tell them to work in pairs to think of positive adjectives for each member of the group and to write the adjective and name on the sticky labels.
● Cut out each label and give them to the appropriate child.
● Ask everyone to choose their favourite label, stand up, say it, stick it on their shirt and wear it during the day.
● The remaining labels can be stuck around the room as affirmatives for the children.

# FAMOUS ARTISTS

**THINKING SKILL:** reasoning
**SUBJECT LINK:** art
**LEARNING LINK:** kinaesthetic
**ORGANISATION:** pairs
**RESOURCES:** sets of familiar paintings for each pair, for example *Sunflowers* by Vincent van Gogh, *Mona Lisa* by Leonardo de Vinci, any of the *Campbell's Soup Can* series by Andy Warhol (blank out the name of the artist and title if you use postcards); labels with the name of each artist and of each painting; pencil and paper

## WHAT TO DO

● Ask the children to look at the set of pictures. Do they recognise the paintings?
● They should try to match the correct artist with the correct painting.
● Remind them to write down the name of the painting, the artist and put the picture with their answer.
● They share their answers with other pairs, and talk about their reasons for matching artists and titles to a picture. How can they tell a piece of art is by a particular artist?

## NOW TRY THIS

Limit the choice to pieces by one artist, Monet for example. Ask the children to match the pictures and titles. The children could discuss an artist's style and look at how paintings may be similar or different.

# SPORT LINKS

**THINKING SKILL:** reasoning
**SUBJECT LINK:** PE
**ORGANISATION:** individuals
**RESOURCES:** felt-tipped pens and paper; photographs of different sports balls, such as a netball, rugby ball, tennis ball, table tennis ball displayed on the board (or draw them); the words *team*, *individual* and *doubles* written randomly on the board; numbers that can be related to sports written randomly on the board, such as 7, 15, 2, 4

## WHAT TO DO

● Who likes playing games?
● On the board are a variety of sports balls and different numbers.
● Do you know what the numbers stand for? Can you link each ball with the appropriate number? Write down the sport and the number of people who make up that team. Say whether it is a team, individual or doubles sport.
● Compare your answers with a partner. Talk about why you matched particular numbers to each sport.

## NOW TRY THIS

Write down as many sports as you can think of. How many people are involved in each sport? How many events are there at the Olympic Games? What does pentathlon mean? What does triathlon mean?

> **ANSWERS**
> 7 in a netball team, 15 in a rugby squad, 2 or 4 in a tennis or table tennis team.

# SHOE ARTIST

**THINKING SKILL:** creative thinking, enquiry
**SUBJECT LINK:** art
**LEARNING LINK:** tactile
**ORGANISATION:** pairs
**RESOURCES:** pencil or charcoal and paper; a collection of different shoes such as slipper, Wellington boot, school shoe, stiletto, army boot, trainer

## WHAT TO DO

● Pick a shoe. Put it on the table in front of you.
● You have one minute to examine this shoe. Take a picture of it in your head, feel the grooves and observe the details of straps, lines, laces, scuffed bits, and colour.
● Put the shoe back on the table. Cover the shoes with a cloth.
● You have four minutes to draw your shoe from memory.
● Uncover the shoes. Compare your drawing with the real shoe.
● What did you find? Which parts of the shoe were easiest to remember? Why?

## NOW TRY THIS

Write down as many different types of shoe as you can. When would you wear them?

# HEALTHY EATING

**THINKING SKILL:** information processing
**SUBJECT LINK:** art, design and technology, PSHE
**LEARNING LINK:** kinaesthetic
**ORGANISATION:** pairs
**RESOURCES:** paper plates for each group; pens and felt-tipped pens

## WHAT TO DO

● You are going to prepare a healthy meal for another pair. What did you have for supper last night? Breakfast this morning?
● What are healthy foods? What types of food are needed to make a balanced diet?
● Using the paper plate, you need to make up a balanced plate of food for one day.
● What are the most important foods you need? Write down or draw these foods.
● Share your ideas with another pair. Did they divide their plate the same way?

## NOW TRY THIS

**1.** Discuss various words, such as carbohydrates, vitamins, minerals, fat, and sugars.
**2.** Divide the plate like a pie chart. Each food type is represented on one segment. Which is the biggest segment?
**3.** What are your favourite vegetables? What are your least favourite?

# COLOUR MIXING

**THINKING SKILL:** evaluation
**SUBJECT LINK:** art
**ORGANISATION:** pairs
**RESOURCES:** a number of blank Venn diagrams for each pair, and one drawn on the board; colouring pencils

## WHAT TO DO

● Tell the children that they are going to experiment with colour mixing to see what different colours they can make.
● They need to decide which colour goes in each part of the diagram.

● Do one example of a colour Venn diagram on the board. For example, colour in the two outer parts of the circles red and blue, and the overlap purple.
● What other colour combinations can they think of? Encourage them to colour in as many different diagrams as they can. They can start with any two colours.
● Compare everyone's diagram. Which mixed colours work best and which are less successful?

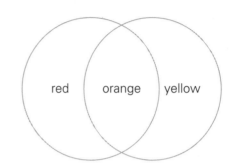

# PATTERNS

**THINKING SKILL:** evaluation, creative thinking
**LEARNING LINK:** tactile
**SUBJECT LINK:** art
**ORGANISATION:** pairs
**RESOURCES:** pencils, colouring pencils; paper; the following patterns drawn on the board (horizontal lines, vertical lines, dots or spheres)

## WHAT TO DO

● Look at the patterns on the board.
● Which one is different? Why?
● Draw a set of three patterns on your paper. One of them should be different from the other two. You could draw two patterns with straight lines and one with wiggly lines, or two patterns with circles and one with triangles.
● Swap drawings with your partner. Can they spot the pattern that is different?

## NOW TRY THIS

**1.** Make up patterns using colours. For example, two patterns could use primary colours and one secondary colours.
**2.** Create four or five patterns of which one or two are odd ones out.

# FLOATING FINGER

**THINKING SKILL:** enquiry
**SUBJECT LINK:** PE
**LEARNING LINK:** kinaesthetic
**ORGANISATION:** individual
**RESOURCES:** none required

## WHAT TO DO

● How many fingers do you have? How many thumbs?
● You can make another finger float in front of your eyes to make nine fingers by concentrating hard!
● Find a place to stand facing the wall.
● Hold your two hands in a fist shape facing each other in front of your face at eye level.
● Put out your two index fingers, pointing at each other.
● Focus on the wall several feet behind your fingers – what happens?
● What happens when you pull your fingers apart and together?
● This is called an illusion!
● Why do you think this happens?

## NOW TRY THIS

If you focus on your fingers, instead of the wall, what happens?

### ANSWER
By focusing on the wall, the two fingers in the foreground incorrectly overlap, producing a stereogram with the floating finger.

# ROMAN COUNTING

**THINKING SKILL:** reasoning
**SUBJECT LINK:** history
**LEARNING LINK:** auditory
**ORGANISATION:** pairs
**RESOURCES:** paper and pencil; roman numerals written on the board: I, II, III, IV, V, VI, VII, VIII, IX, X

## WHAT TO DO

● Ask everyone to think of a number between one and ten.

● Do they know what a Roman numeral is? Do they know what their number is in Roman numerals?
● Ask them what number five looks like in Roman numerals.
● Ask them to think of a grandfather clock, and picture the numerals. Draw a big circle on the board and work out where the numerals should be.
● Can they see a pattern in the numerals?
● Read out some addition and subtraction sums. They listen, and write the sums and answers in Roman numerals.

## NOW TRY THIS

Make the sums more challenging by including multiplication and division.

# CODE BREAKERS

**THINKING SKILL:** reasoning
**SUBJECT LINK:** literacy
**LEARNING LINK:** kinaesthetic
**ORGANISATION:** pairs
**RESOURCES:** pen and paper; write the following codes on the board:

| | |
|---|---|
| 19, 20, 21, 4, 25 | 8, 1, 18, 4 |
| 20, 8, 9, 14, 11 | 5, 1, 19, 25 |

## WHAT TO DO

● Tell the pairs they are going to be code breakers.
● Ask, *If a = 1 and b = 2 what does c =?*
● If each letter of the alphabet represents a number and z = 26, ask them to work out the code for each letter.
● Write these down. Ask the children to break the codes to uncover the secret message.
● Can they make up a code of their own for their partner to decipher?

### ANSWER
Study hard, think easy.

# READY STEADY GO

**THINKING SKILL:** information processing
**SUBJECT LINK:** PE
**LEARNING LINK:** kinaesthetic
**ORGANISATION:** individual
**RESOURCES:** concept map

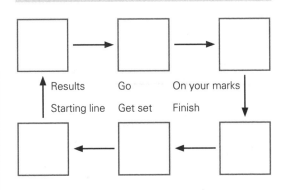

Results    Go    On your marks
Starting line    Get set    Finish

## WHAT TO DO

● Imagine you are about to run a race.
● Where do you start?
● Think about the sequence of a running race. Write the words in the appropriate squares, in the correct order.
● Does it matter which square you start in?

## NOW TRY THIS

Think about another activity such as cleaning your teeth or getting dressed. Write down the sequence of events.

# MAKE-ME-UP

**THINKING SKILL:** information processing
**SUBJECT LINK:** history
**LEARNING LINK:** tactile
**ORGANISATION:** pairs
**RESOURCES:** a variety of labels written on the board such as: red wine, red felt-tipped pen, ash, marmalade, clay, mud, powdered chalk, plant dye, grass, tree bark, sand, beer, honey, whale bone; real examples of the items too, if available; a picture of a Roman woman for each pair

## WHAT TO DO

● Look at the words on the board. Guess which materials were used by Roman women to make-up their faces. Did they want to look pale or dark-skinned?

● Copy the labels off the board. Put arrows to where you think the women put these materials. If you think they put clay on their cheeks, write clay and draw an arrow to connect clay with cheeks.
● Ask each other questions such as, What might whale bone be used for now?
● Can you find a purpose for each label even if it was not used in Roman make-up?

## NOW TRY THIS

Try this matching activity for make-up in the Elizabethan age, or foods that people ate in Roman times.

> **ANSWERS**
> To colour their lips and cheeks red they used red wine sediment or a plant dye called fucus.
> Eyelids were darkened with ash.
> They whitened their faces and arms with powdered chalk.

# WHO'S HE?

**THINKING SKILL:** creative thinking
**SUBJECT LINK:** history
**ORGANISATION:** pairs
**RESOURCES:** pens; big sheets of paper; *Henry VIII* written on the board

## WHAT TO DO

● Point to the words Henry VIII. Ask someone to say them aloud.
● Ask the children if anyone knows who he was. Listen to their suggestions.
● The pairs have to write Henry VIII in the middle of the page and write words or draw things that they link to Henry VIII.
● They can use words to describe his appearance (big), status (important, king) or phrases associated with his life (lots of wives, chopped people's heads off).

## NOW TRY THIS

Provide a list of words. Ask the children to draw the sort of king those words could describe.

# INDIGESTION

**THINKING SKILL:** enquiry
**SUBJECT LINK:** science
**LEARNING LINK:** tactile
**ORGANISATION:** individuals or pairs
**RESOURCES:** pen and paper

## WHAT TO DO

● Imagine there is an animal that likes eating anything. He lives under the bed and munches his way through anything he sees in the bedroom. When he gets terrible indigestion his owner takes him to the vet and the vet takes an x-ray of his stomach. What does he see?

● Draw an outline of an animal on your piece of paper.

● Write a list of all the things that he can digest, like toast, biscuit crumbs and sweets.

● Write a list of all the things he cannot digest, like coins, a belt, buttons, a comb.

● The foods are digestible so the vet won't see them in the x-ray. He will see the indigestible things. Draw these in the animal's outline.

● Compare your drawings.

# I SEE HOW YOU FEEL

**THINKING SKILL:** information processing
**SUBJECT LINK:** PSHE
**LEARNING LINK:** auditory
**ORGANISATION:** whole class, individual
**RESOURCES:** a large, random selection of magazine photos

## WHAT TO DO

● The children sit or stand in a circle. Spread out the photos in the middle.

● Explain that sometimes it's difficult to say how you're feeling. It can help to have a picture.

● Ask them to look at the pictures.

● They should choose two or three that they like and that explain how they feel – for example, they might like a picture with lots of red because they feel angry, or one of an animal because they love their pet.

● Ask them in turn to step forward and pick up their picture. If someone has already taken it, they choose another.

● Go round the circle. Ask them to say why they chose their picture. If they don't want to, they say, pass.

# ZOOM THINKING

**THINKING SKILL:** enquiry
**SUBJECT LINK:** science
**ORGANISATION:** whole class, pairs
**RESOURCES:** *Zoom* by Istvan Banyai (paperback – Puffin Books, hardback – Viking Children's Books); a picture of the earth from space; a magnifying glass

## WHAT TO DO

● A zoom lens on a camera makes things appear closer than they are.

● When you zoom in on a picture, you can see a small part of it in detail.

● Look at *Zoom* by Istvan Banyai to see how this works.

● Have a go at zooming in on various things – using your imagination.

● Imagine you are in a hot air balloon, floating over the school:
  ● Zoom in on a window.
  ● Zoom in on the classroom.
  ● Zoom in on yourself.
  ● Zoom in on your face.
  ● Zoom in on your nose.
  ● Zoom in on your skin.
  ● Zoom in on the pores of your skin.

● Now work with a partner. Start in outer space, looking at the earth. Talk about the different stages of zooming in. What would you see? How far can you go?

## NOW TRY THIS

Think about other places to zoom in on. For example, look out of the window, look at the floor, look at a forest.

# ANYTHING BUT 'SAID'

**THINKING SKILL:** enquiry, evaluation
**SUBJECT LINK:** literacy
**ORGANISATION:** pair
**RESOURCES:** felt-tipped pens; paper

## WHAT TO DO

● Tell the children that when you are speaking, you are saying something. Emphasise the verb *to say*. Remind them that said is a verb that is a doing or action word.

● Explain that there are lots of ways to say something. Ask them to write down as many words as they can use instead of said, such as shouted or answered.

● Ask pairs for their answers. Write the different responses on the board.

● Give the children a selection of situations. Ask them to decide which speaking verb would be best to use when you want:

  ● to warn someone who is about to fall down a hole

  ● your baby brother to go to sleep with a song

  ● to find out which way to go from a policeman

  ● to buy a train ticket at a noisy station

  ● your mum to give you pocket money.

## NOW TRY THIS

**1.** Add an auditory element by asking volunteers to say alternative words to *said* in the style of their chosen word, for example, they can say she questioned in a quizzical tone.
**2.** Try this game with other verbs, such as *to walk*.

# WORDS WITHIN WORDS

**THINKING SKILL:** creative thinking
**SUBJECT LINK:** music
**ORGANISATION:** pairs
**RESOURCES:** pen and paper; the word musicianship written on the board

## WHAT TO DO

● Point to the word musicianship written on the board. Ask a child to read it aloud.

● Can they find a word they recognise in this word?

● Tell them to look for and write down as many words as they can, using the letters from the word musicianship.

● They can only use the letters in the word to make new words and cannot have proper nouns, so they cannot record names of people, places or things.

> **ANSWERS**
> For example: ship, musician, an, sun, pin, shin, shins, in.

## NOW TRY THIS

Ask the children to find as many instruments as they can starting with *A* and then move onto *B*, and so on.

# LADDER LEARNING

**THINKING SKILL:** information processing
**SUBJECT LINK:** literacy
**ORGANISATION:** pairs
**RESOURCES:** a copy of a ladder on A4 paper for each pair; pencils; a ladder drawn on the board; a list of words on the board as starter words, for example, help, way, book, friend

## WHAT TO DO

● Point to the ladder on the board. Tell the children that ladder learning is a great way to add bits to words to make them longer.

● In this way, they can extend their vocabulary. If the word *hope* is written on the first rung, how many words can they make from that word, adding letters at the beginning and at the end, such as hopeful, hopefully, hopeless, hopelessly.

● Who can make the longest word? Which rung have they reached? Ask the children to compare their ladder with another pair. Draw another ladder. Write a starter word on the bottom rung and ask them to make new words for each rung.

## NOW TRY THIS

Introduce the words prefix and suffix. Give the children a long word written on the top rung of the ladder. Ask them to take off letters from the start or end of the word. How far down the ladder can they get? For example, beautifully, beautiful, beauty, fully, full.

# DREAM MACHINE

**THINKING SKILL:** enquiry, creative thinking
**SUBJECT LINK:** general
**LEARNING LINK:** auditory
**ORGANISATION:** whole class
**RESOURCES:** clouds drawn on the board

## WHAT TO DO

● There is a special dream machine that takes you to a real or imaginary place from your past.

● Draw some clouds on your paper and start dreaming, close your eyes.

● Where do you go? Is it a house, a place you visited on holiday or a spooky castle? Write down your thoughts in the clouds.

● What is the scene in your dream? Is it mysterious or sad, frightening or welcoming?

● What are you doing? Are you watching television, playing with someone, running away from danger?

● Who do you meet there? Are they friendly? Scary?

● Do you feel anxious, or comfortable and safe?

● Use these dream clouds as a framework for a story.

## NOW TRY THIS

**1.** The dream machine has two special buttons: Nightmare and Escape.

**2.** If you press Nightmare, your dream reverses – anything nice turns nasty, anything nasty turns nice.

**3.** Escape wakes you up.

**4.** Play with the buttons and see what happens to your dream.

# BEHIND THE SCENES

**THINKING SKILL:** information processing
**SUBJECT LINK:** PSHE
**ORGANISATION:** whole class
**RESOURCES:** video/DVD player; a one-minute clip from any children's file showing characters interacting and things happening in the background (for example, scenes from *Finding Nemo* (Pixar) and *Monsters Inc* (Pixar))

## WHAT TO DO

● You are going to watch a one-minute clip of a DVD.

● Usually your eyes would be drawn to the main characters and the action.

● Try to ignore the characters and action. Look at the background – the things you don't normally notice – something on the wall, the view through a window, an object at the edge of the screen.

● Your teacher will play the clip twice.

● Look hard. Remember what you notice.

● Which things did lots of people notice? Which things were less easy?

# CLOSE-UP

**THINKING SKILL:** reasoning
**SUBJECT LINK:** art
**ORGANISATION:** groups of three or four
**RESOURCES:** photographs for each group – a close-up of a particular image, plus a clue to the image on a label or the back of the photograph (for example, close-up of an ear – clue: a body part, close-up of a finger nail – clue: you all have these)

## WHAT TO DO

● Look at a close-up of a photograph.

● Your task is to work out what the whole picture is.

## NOW TRY THIS

Choose an object in the classroom – which part would you show in close-up to make it hard to recognise?

# SORT IT OUT

**THINKING SKILL:** information processing
**SUBJECT LINK:** mathematics
**ORGANISATION:** whole class, individuals
**RESOURCES:** a whiteboard and pen (or paper and pencil) for each child

## WHAT TO DO

- We use Venn diagrams to sort things out.
- With two circles in the diagram, we need to ask two questions.
- We are going to sort some numbers out, but we are only interested in numbers that don't fit in the Venn diagram – they'll go in the space outside.

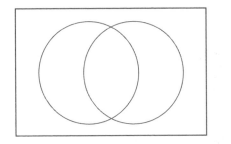

- Here are the numbers we're going to sort: 1, 3, 7, 9, 14, 24, 33, 44, 58, 67, 102, 174.
- Even numbers go in the left circle and numbers with only straight lines go in the right circle.
- What numbers go in the middle?
- What numbers don't go in either circle?
- Copy the Venn diagram. Write down only those numbers that go outside both circles.
- Remember that there are usually things that don't fit into any Venn diagram – it depends on the questions asked.

# WHY, MR ARTIST?

**THINKING SKILL:** reasoning, enquiry
**SUBJECT LINK:** science, PHSE
**LEARNING LINK:** auditory
**ORGANISATION:** whole class, pairs, fours
**RESOURCES:** a piece of artwork that includes people, for example *Bathers at Asnières* by Georges Seurat

## WHAT TO DO

- Make sure you can see the painting.
- Your challenge is to think up different questions to ask the artist about the painting.
- Then you will try to answer them yourselves.

- Look at the painting in silence for a minute – think up a question. For example, *Why are they wearing hats?*
- Tell your partner your question and listen to their question. Think up two more questions together.
- Join with another pair. The first pair ask their questions. The second pair have to come up with answers.
- For example, *Why are they wearing hats? It's a hot day… Because it was fashionable.*
- The second pair ask their questions and the first pair reply.

# SLEEPING SATELLITE

**THINKING SKILL:** information processing, enquiry
**SUBJECT LINK:** geography, ICT
**ORGANISATION:** whole class, pairs
**RESOURCES:** a satellite/aerial photograph – use a hard copy or display it in on an interactive whiteboard

## WHAT TO DO

- Show the children the aerial or satellite photograph, saying where the place is.
- Tell them it was taken from a satellite many kilometres above Earth. Point out one or two features.
- Give them two minutes (in silence) to identify any two of these four things:
  - a (geographic or physical) feature that stands out (even if they don't know what it is)
  - something they can recognise
  - something they don't recognise
  - any sort of pattern they notice.
- Now ask them to take two minutes to discuss their observations in pairs.

### NOW TRY THIS

Use blobs of Blu-Tack™ or pencils/wipe off markers to mark features that are the same – for example, all churches/all trees.

## BIG BANG

**THINKING SKILL:** enquiry
**SUBJECT LINK:** mathematics
**ORGANISATION:** individual
**RESOURCES:** a 'big bang' drawing displayed

### WHAT TO DO

● Scientists believe that the universe began with a big bang, when everything exploded outwards.

● They say that this is still happening – everything is moving out from the middle.

● We will use this idea to think about numbers.

● If the number in the middle of the picture has exploded and made all the fragments on the outside, what number was in the middle before it exploded?

● There are lots of different answers to this question.

● How will you combine all the numbers? Will you add them up, or do something different?

● How many different combinations can you think of? What are the largest and smallest numbers you can think of?

## SHAPE UP

**THINKING SKILL:** evaluation
**SUBJECT LINK:** design and technology
**ORGANISATION:** whole class
**RESOURCES:** none required

### WHAT TO DO

● Explain that Mr Geo likes getting new things that no one else has.

● He wants the children to make him an 'all-new-shape' which:
*has some corners*
*has some curves*
*looks good*
*has some straight lines.*

● Write the criteria on the board and draw some examples of possible new shapes:

● Ask them to spend a couple of minutes in pairs deciding which shape will be the best one for Mr Geo.

> **ANSWERS**
> There is no right answer here – the challenge comes in justifying choices and realising that Mr Geo's requirements are not very clear – they can have more than one interpretation.

## PICTURE MY SHAPE

**THINKING SKILL:** enquiry
**SUBJECT LINK:** mathematics
**ORGANISATION:** whole class, sitting in a circle
**RESOURCES:** a selection of 2D and 3D shapes; paper and a pencil for each child

### WHAT TO DO

● Display the shapes in the middle of the class.

● Remind the class what the differences are between 2D and 3D shapes.

● Check that they know the relevant vocabulary.

● Review the shape-related vocabulary with which they are already familiar, for example, corner, vertex, side, face.

● Choose one person to approach the shapes.

● Ask them to mentally choose a shape but not tell anyone which one.

● The child must focus on this shape and look carefully at its properties.

● Once they have the shape pictured in their mind, they must describe it to the class, giving as much detail as possible.

● As the mystery shape is being described, the rest of the class must try to visualise it.

● In order to help the class picture the shape, they can draw it as it is being described.

● As children think they've worked out what it is, they put up two thumbs. Once the shape has been positively identified, another child can choose a shape.

### NOW TRY THIS
Choose two shapes and describe common properties – for example, a square and a rectangle. Describe four sides, four corners. The class now try to identify and visualise a pair of shapes.

# SQUIGGLE THINKING

**THINKING SKILL:** creative thinking
**SUBJECT LINK:** general
**ORGANISATION:** whole class
**RESOURCES:** chalk/pen; a board

### WHAT TO DO
● Explain that the human mind can fill in gaps and join up shapes to make something new.
● Draw simple, random shapes, like the one below:

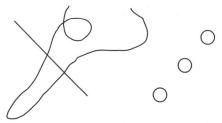

● What do the children see?
● They will create many different results. For example, they could see a needle, thread and three holes in some fabric, or a bird balancing a pencil on its beak next to three eggs.

# DESIGN IN COMFORT

**THINKING SKILL:** reasoning
**SUBJECT LINK:** design and technology
**ORGANISATION:** whole class
**RESOURCES:** vacant regular school chair; A3 sheet of paper and pencil

### WHAT TO DO
● The head teacher has asked your class to design a new school chair.
● It needs to be comfortable and have one special feature.
● The special feature is something you must decide as a class – and have a good reason.

● You must consider improvements that could be made to the existing chair.
● Think about the shape, design, material and overall look, the need for the design to be practical but also stylish and modern.
● Select one person to draw your design on the A3 sheet.
● When you have an idea, put your hand up and share it with the artist.
● Together, as a class, build up the image of the chair.

# THINKING ABOUT THINKING

**THINKING SKILL:** evaluation
**SUBJECT LINK:** general
**ORGANISATION:** individual
**RESOURCES:** sheet with illustration of a simple outline of a brain; pen/pencil and colours for each child

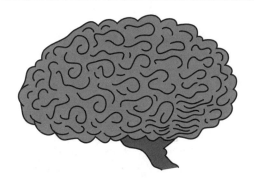

### WHAT TO DO
● We do a lot of thinking every day while we're learning.
● What do you think is happening in your head when you're thinking?
● Spend just ten minutes colouring, drawing and writing on the sheet. Think about all the different things you do in the day. Draw pictures to show what is happening in your head during different times of the day.
● Be creative.
● Talk about your ideas with your partner.

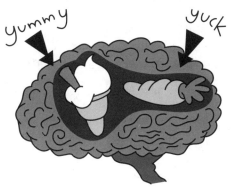

# THINKING KNIFE

**THINKING SKILL:** enquiry
**SUBJECT LINK:** geography
**ORGANISATION:** individual
**RESOURCES:** a pencil and paper for each child (it would be useful to do the first example on an interactive whiteboard)

## WHAT TO DO

● Explain that a thinking knife is a great thing to have. It's like a real knife, but instead of cutting things, it cuts up ideas!
● Use a thinking knife to demonstrate cutting an idea linked to geography into smaller bits, leaving the main points of the idea. For example: Traffic congestion can affect the environment.
● Cut away 'can affect' (not the key idea) to leave Traffic congestion/the environment.
● Cut up what's left: Traffic/congestion/environment.
● Explain that these are the key concepts from the statement.

## NOW TRY THIS

**1.** Ask the children to use a thinking knife on some of these:

*The three longest rivers in the UK are the Severn, the Thames and the Trent.*
*The largest mountain range in Europe is the Alps.*
*Water and wind can change the landscape by erosion.*
*Places can change when more people move to live there.*
*We can improve our environment by recycling and reusing waste.*

**2.** Discuss why they sliced in certain places.

# WORDY SCIENCE

**THINKING SKILL:** creative thinking
**SUBJECT LINK:** science
**ORGANISATION:** individual
**RESOURCES:** words relating to science, written on the board: electricity, force, teeth, light, air, water, lungs, heart, flower, ice, steam, sound, the Sun

## WHAT TO DO

● Look at the words on the board; they are all related to science.
● Choose one of the words and copy it down. Add things to it to help you understand more about it. Don't change the letters, but use them in a picture of something to do with that bit of science.
● Here's an example, on electricity:

# IMAGINARY ANIMALS

**THINKING SKILL:** information processing
**SUBJECT LINK:** science
**ORGANISATION:** whole class, individuals
**RESOURCES:** picture of, or ideally a real, animal

## WHAT TO DO

● Look closely at this animal.
● Now close your eyes. Try to picture it in your mind.
● Open your eyes and take another look.
● Close your eyes. Imagine it with an extra head, extra leg, a different colour, how would it sound if it spoke, a different type of skin… and so on.
● Now imagine it as it is normally.
● Open your eyes and draw what you imagined.

# THE ANYTHING MACHINE

**THINKING SKILL:** creative thinking
**SUBJECT LINK:** design and technology
**ORGANISATION:** individuals, pairs
**RESOURCES:** copies of the Anything Machine diagram:

## WHAT TO DO

- The Anything Machine is very special. You can put anything in, it can do anything, but you never quite know what will come out.
- Here's an example:
  - You could set the machine to make things longer
  - You could put in a dog, a shoe that doesn't fit anymore, a clock, yourself and your holiday
  - What comes out? (a long dog, a shoe that fits, a long clock, a taller you and a longer holiday).
- Invent your own Anything Machine.
- Decide what it will do. For example, it could make things hairy, make a copy, cut things in half, make things blue.
- Here are the things to put in – a pencil, a watch, a pizza, a mouse, your best friend, your bedroom, a football, a CD-ROM, a book, the school. What can your machine do with them?
- Try some ideas of your own.

# ICT WEB

**THINKING SKILL:** reasoning
**SUBJECT LINK:** ICT
**ORGANISATION:** individuals, pairs
**RESOURCES:** paper and pencil for each child; a list of words linked to ICT, written on the board (adapt the words to suit the children's experience): computer; DVD; camcorder, mobile phone, database, animation, MP3, JPEG, robot, printer, internet access, software

## WHAT TO DO

- Look at the words on the board. They are all linked to ICT.
- Copy them on to paper, spreading them out evenly.
- Make at least five connections between pairs of words in three minutes. To make a connection you must use the word *because*. For example:
  - DVD is linked to software because a DVD player needs software to run properly
  - MP3 is linked to internet because you can get MP3 files from the internet.
- In pairs, explain the connections you have made.

## NOW TRY THIS

Your teacher will give out ready-made connections between some words. Why have they been made?

# LITTLE BY LITTLE

**THINKING SKILL:** reasoning
**SUBJECT LINK:** RE
**ORGANISATION:** whole class
**RESOURCES:** words related to RE, written on strips of card (large enough for class to see): Christian, Allah, church, mosque (or words linked to current work); blank card to cover the letters; a whiteboard and pen (or paper and pencil) for each child

## WHAT TO DO

- Tell the children that you are going to reveal a word linked to work on RE – one letter at a time.
- They have to guess and write down what they think the word is each time a letter is revealed.
- With the word covered completely, they make a guess at what the word could be. If support is needed, say how many letters are in the word, but otherwise give them the challenge of guessing the word.
- Reveal the first letter. The children write down what they think the word is.
- Reveal the next letter. They write down another word if they've changed their mind.
- Keep going until the word is obvious. Ask the children to share their guesses.

## NOW TRY THIS

1. Uncover letters in a random order instead of uncovering them in sequence, or uncover them backwards.
2. Uncover pictures instead of words. The children have to guess what the picture shows.

# WHERE ON EARTH?

**THINKING SKILL:** creative thinking
**SUBJECT LINK:** geography
**LEARNING LINK:** auditory, tactile
**ORGANISATION:** groups
**RESOURCES:** any selection of objects – about five per group

## WHAT TO DO

- Explain that different objects are found in different places and can give information about that place.
- Give each group five objects. Ask them to imagine/create the place where these objects came from.
- Here's an example:

> Objects: match, blank book, leaf, pencil, set of earphones.
> The place where these objects were found is a desert island full of trees (the leaf). A plane has crashed and a boy is the only survivor (earphones from the plane). He is writing his diary (blank book, pencil) in case he is never rescued – the people who find his skeleton will know what happened. His only hope is to light a signal fire with his last match… (the match)

## NOW TRY THIS

Start with a photo of a place. Ask the children to name five objects that might be found there.

# CREATE A CD-ROM COVER

**THINKING SKILL:** creative thinking
**SUBJECT LINK:** ICT
**LEARNING LINK:** tactile
**ORGANISATION:** pairs
**RESOURCES:** examples of CD covers; a computer with a drawing program per pair

## WHAT TO DO

- Show the children a selection of CD covers, but keep one cover out of view.
- Encourage a discussion about the images used and the wording/fonts.
- Ask what effect they think the cover might have on someone coming in to buy a CD.
- Give them the title of the CD that was left out of view.
- The task for the children is to design a CD cover based on this title.

- Set simple criteria – for example, the CD cover must include:

> Group or artist name
> Title
> Only two colours
> One face
> One other image

- Once the covers are designed, invite the children to compare them and to select their favourite.
- Show them the original.

## NOW TRY THIS

Repeat this activity with book covers.

# FOOD CHAIN

**THINKING SKILL:** reasoning
**SUBJECT LINK:** science
**ORGANISATION:** pairs and whole class
**RESOURCES:** an A3 sheet of paper (attached to the wall/board); pencils; A5 sheets and Blu-Tack™; a list of animals and plants written on the board: spider, carrot, fly, lion, bird, snake, cat, duck, grass, hen, cow, pig, human, whale, minnow, cod, plankton, seagull, shrimp, crab, seaweed, corn, worm, ant, deer, frog, eagle, owl, mouse, rat, otter

## WHAT TO DO

- Explain that a food chain is the order in which animals eat each other – for example, little fish eat insects, large fish eat little fish, humans eat large fish.
- Present the list. Ask the children, in pairs, to organise three or more animals/plants into a food chain – thinking about whether one animal can eat the other.
- The aim is to get the longest chain.
- As a class, share chains.
- Ask them to close their eyes and visualise a food chain. They need to consider where the chain starts and where it finishes.

> Note: where necessary be sensitive to those children who are vegetarian and/or whose beliefs exclude the consumption of certain foods.

## NOW TRY THIS

Once a chain has been drawn, cover up one part of it. Discuss what would happen to the chain if the covered up part was missing – if the chain was broken.

# A FAMILY LINE

**THINKING SKILL:** information processing
**SUBJECT LINK:** PHSE, RE
**LEARNING LINK:** tactile
**ORGANISATION:** individual
**RESOURCES:** for each child: an A4 sheet of paper and a pencil

## WHAT TO DO

- Think about your family for a few minutes.
- Close your eyes. Imagine yourself in a family photograph.
- Open your eyes and in the middle of the sheet, draw a picture of your face – however, you may only use a single line for each feature – one line for an eye, one for a mouth, and so on. This will make your picture quick to draw.
- On either side of your drawing, draw up to three members of your family in the same way.

- Choose the people carefully. They are the people you consider to be special to you.

## NOW TRY THIS

Count the number of lines you have used in total. Redraw the same picture but with five less lines – which features did you leave out?

# A CLASSROOM COLLAGE

**THINKING SKILL:** creative thinking
**SUBJECT LINK:** geography
**LEARNING LINK:** tactile, kinaesthetic
**ORGANISATION:** individuals
**RESOURCES:** A5 sheet folded in four; pencils; a large sheet of paper; Blu-Tack™; scissors

## WHAT TO DO

- Attach a large sheet of paper to the wall.
- Give each child an A5 sheet of paper and a pencil and ask them to fold it into four, then open it out.

- Ask them one by one to find a space in the classroom and to walk into it.
- Wait until everyone is in place. Ensure that they are well spaced out and can see different parts of the room.
- Now focus their minds on what they can see in their immediate area.
- Ask them to draw four things that they see – one in each quarter of their sheet.
- Give them only a few minutes to complete this task.
- When they have finished, get them to sit down again.
- Explain that they are now going to make a collage of the classroom.
- They should cut out their four images and stick them onto the paper – the only rule is that each image must be next to at least one other.

## NOW TRY THIS

Repeat the collage process in different rooms and outside.

# MOVE ALONG PLEASE

**THINKING SKILL:** evaluation
**SUBJECT LINK:** design and technology
**ORGANISATION:** individual
**RESOURCES:** photographs or drawings of a bridge, a road, an escalator, stairs, a lift, a car, a plane, a skateboard, shoes, a bike, a cycle path and other man-made designs related to travel

## WHAT TO DO

- Show the children a selection of pictures of items designed and built to help people travel.
- Each child must pick two items, with something in common, for example, escalators and stairs both go up and down.
- Share a selection of the choices.
- Ask them to think up a situation when one of their items is more useful than the other – for example, stairs are better than an escalator when there's a power cut.
- Ask them to think of a situation when the other item would be preferred – for example, an escalator is better when someone has a broken leg.

## NOW TRY THIS

Ask them to pick three items with something in common and then compare them – when would each be preferred?

# VISUAL LEARNING

## IF...THEN SCIENCE

**THINKING SKILL:** reasoning
**SUBJECT LINK:** science
**ORGANISATION:** pairs
**RESOURCES:** a mixed-up 'If...then' list:

| If | Then |
| --- | --- |
| You throw a stone into the air | It's a fair test |
| You join a bulb and battery in a complete circuit | It will turn into ice |
| You change only one thing at once in an experiment | You will be healthy |
| You do more exercise | The bulb will light up |
| You eat a balanced diet | The plants will die |
| You put plants in the dark | It always pushes back |
| You put water in the freezer | It will fall back down to earth |
| You put sugar into very hot water | Your heart beats faster |
| You push something | It makes a shadow |
| You block out light | It will dissolve |

### WHAT TO DO

● 'If...then' is a great way to glue ideas together.
● The 'If' happens first and makes the 'Then' happen.
● Give each pair a mixed-up list of 'If' and 'Then'.
● The children discuss the ideas in pairs and match the 'If' to the correct 'Then'.
● They don't need to write anything down.

## MINE'S BETTER THAN YOURS

**THINKING SKILL:** evaluation
**SUBJECT LINK:** mathematics
**ORGANISATION:** pairs
**RESOURCES:** a pen and paper; ten numbers written on the board (suited to the class mathematics level)

### WHAT TO DO

● Your teacher will write ten numbers on the board.
● In pairs, choose one number and write it down.

● Without showing your partner, make your number into something else by drawing on to it (for example, 3 could become a snake).
● After a couple of minutes, show your partner what you have drawn. Justify your creation by saying, *My_____ is better than yours_____ because...*
● You only gets three turns at saying this each – so think carefully.

### NOW TRY THIS

**1.** Try drawing a different number from your partner. Who has the better picture?
**2.** Pick a number without telling your partner. Ask him or her to guess which number you started with.
**3.** Instead of numbers, use the mathematical symbols: <,>, -, =, + or use letters.

## HOW ABOUT...

**THINKING SKILL:** reasoning, creative thinking
**SUBJECT LINK:** science
**LEARNING LINK:** auditory
**ORGANISATION:** individual
**RESOURCES:** a set of equipment used to carry out science experiments, for example, a thermometer, a newtonmeter, a stopwatch, a test tube, a magnifying glass, a freezer (picture of), a cooker (picture of), a battery, wire, and so on; a selection of items from the school environment, for example, grass, paper, scissors, shoes, pens, a sunflower, a sandwich box

### WHAT TO DO

● Scientific discoveries often come about by chance. Can you make a chance discovery?
● Look carefully at these pieces of equipment and at these items from around the school.
● Pick one from each group and put both into a 'How about' sentence – just to see what happens.
● Here are a couple of examples: *How about using a thermometer to measure the temperature of a sunflower... How about using a stop watch to see how long it takes to make one scissor cut...*
● Share ideas – which are the funniest? The most interesting?

### NOW TRY THIS

Combine two pieces of equipment and invent a new experiment.

# HOW WOULD YOU ACT?

**THINKING SKILL:** creative thinking
**SUBJECT LINK:** PSHE, RE
**LEARNING LINK:** auditory
**ORGANISATION:** pairs
**RESOURCES:** sentences on strips of paper

Examples of possible situations to give:

*I don't like your friend. I don't want you to play with them anymore.*
*Let's go and take that chocolate bar from the shop. No one is looking.*
*If you want to be cool, try this cigarette.*
*Don't bother doing your homework. I never do.*
*Let's bunk off school today and go into town.*
*I know you don't know me but I'm a friend of your Mum. She asked me to give you a lift home. Jump in.*
*You can play with us but your mate can't.*

## WHAT TO DO

● Ask each pair to label themselves 'A' or 'B'.
● Give all of the 'A's a sentence.
● Tell 'A's that this is the line that they are going to read out to their partner.
● Tell 'B's that they need to listen to what 'A's say and imagine what they would do and say in response.
● Allow time for the children to silently imagine what they would do first, and then a few minutes to practise reading and responding.
● Select a few pairs to show how they responded.
● Swap sentences around. How do different pairs respond?

## NOW TRY THIS

Pairs create a pose, and hold it for five seconds. The rest of the class have to work out which scenario they had.

# MANY HANDS...

**THINKING SKILL:** information processing
**SUBJECT LINK:** science
**ORGANISATION:** groups of six
**RESOURCES:** a pencil/pen; a copy of these questions for each child (or others related to your science work)

*A mirror reflects _____.*
*To light a bulb you need a battery and _____.*
*Shadows are longer at the _____ of the day.*
*Everything is pulled towards the Earth by the force of_____.*
*If you put sugar in hot water, it will _____.*
*Your _____ pumps blood around you body.*
*Smoking is very_____for your health.*
*Plants need light, air and _____to grow.*
*You measure temperature with a _____.*
*A _____ can be used to separate small and large particles.*

## WHAT TO DO

● This is a silent activity.
● When your teacher says *Go*, answer as many of the questions as you can.
● Don't worry about leaving any out.
● When your teacher says *Pass*, hand your sheet to the person on your right and take one from the person on your left.
● Read through the answer, tick it if you agree, put another answer if you don't, and fill in the empty spaces if you can.
● Your teacher will keep saying *Pass* until everyone has had a go at every question sheet.
● When your first sheet is passed back to you, look at it and discuss any different answers.

### ANSWERS

| | | |
|---|---|---|
| Light | Wire | Start or end |
| Gravity | Dissolve | Heart |
| Bad | Water | Thermometer |
| Filter | | |

## COUNTING SYLLABLES

**THINKING SKILL:** information processing
**SUBJECT LINK:** literacy
**ORGANISATION:** pairs
**RESOURCES:** pen and paper

### WHAT TO DO

● Ask who knows what a syllable is.
● Explain that it is like a beat in music, for example, Victoria has four syllables, (Vic-tor-ri-a), Ben has one syllable.
● Practise saying the name. Clap the beat at the same time.
● Ask them to take it in turns to say a name. The other person claps out the syllables and writes the name and number down.

### NOW TRY THIS

They swap partners and say the names of instruments, taking it in turns to clap out the syllables and write the name and number down.

## SOUND EFFECTS

**THINKING SKILL:** evaluation, information processing
**SUBJECT LINK:** music
**ORGANISATION:** pairs
**RESOURCES:** a recording of, for example, a car starting, a baby crying, a phone ringing, brushing teeth, a clock ticking

### WHAT TO DO

● Work with a friend and choose someone to write things down.
● Listen to the sounds. What do you think they are? Write each one down.
● Share your ideas with another group. Discuss the sounds in more detail; for example, *What kind of car made the noise? How old was the crying baby? Was the clock an alarm clock, a grandfather clock or something else?*

## WHAT IF...?

**THINKING SKILL:** creative thinking, reasoning, enquiry
**SUBJECT LINK:** literacy
**ORGANISATION:** groups of three or four
**RESOURCES:** pen and paper; a list of 'What if' questions on the board, for example:

*What if the letter 'a' came at the end of the alphabet?*
*What if there were no pens to write with?*
*What if we could only write with our feet?*
*What if you could only ask questions?*
*What if you could only write in text language?*
*What if spellings did not matter?*
*What if there were no full stops or capital letters?*
*What if you could only write in one exercise book all of your school life?*

### WHAT TO DO

● Think about the following: *What if the world was square? How different would life be? What might be different?*
● Talk about the answers to this and the other 'What if?' questions above. There are not any right or wrong answers.
● Choose someone to write down between five and ten answers for the questions – you can add drawings if you like.

### NOW TRY THIS

**1.** Discuss which answer is the best and which one is the worst, and why.
**2.** Apply the 'What if' questioning to other subjects. Here are some suggestions for science: *What if there were two moons in the sky? What if there was a thunderstorm every day? What if trees only grew in snow? What if the weather could be controlled by people's thoughts?*

# CATERPILLAR THINKING

**THINKING SKILL:** information processing
**SUBJECT LINK:** modern languages
**LEARNING LINK:** auditory
**ORGANISATION:** pairs
**RESOURCES:** a simple outline drawing of a caterpillar on A4 paper, one copy for each pair of children – with five to seven body segments; a list of ways to say hello in different languages

## WHAT TO DO

● How many different words can you think of to say hello, in as many languages as you can think of?
● Discuss the languages we study at school and any others you may know about.
● Fill in each segment of the caterpillar with a different word or phrase. Attempt to say it.
● Think of as many as you can. Compare your findings with another pair.

## NOW TRY THIS

Fill in the caterpillar segments with the days of the week, or other words, in a different language.

# SYNONYM GAME

**THINKING SKILL:** evaluation
**SUBJECT LINK:** literacy
**ORGANISATION:** whole class
**RESOURCES:** whiteboards and pens; a list of adjectives, for example, fat, thin, scary, tiny, pretty, hairy; thesauruses

## WHAT TO DO

● What is a synonym? It's a word that has a similar meaning.
● Here are some examples: sad – miserable, unhappy; quiet – peaceful, still.
● Copy down the adjectives from the board. Think of a synonym for each word. Find as many as you can in three minutes.
● When you have a good list of synonyms, think about how near they are in meaning to the original word. Arrange them in order, writing the ones with the closest meaning nearer to the original word.

● Discuss your findings. Compare results with a partner.

# WHO AM I?

**THINKING SKILL:** evaluation
**SUBJECT LINK:** modern languages
**ORGANISATION:** groups of three or four
**RESOURCES:** a recording of 'Old MacDonald had a Farm'; pencils and paper

## WHAT TO DO

● Tell the children that they are going to listen to a song that they will recognise.
● Ask one child in each group to act as scribe.
● They listen carefully to the song. It can be played as many times as necessary.
● They discuss the name of each animal, agree what it is called in French, and write it down. Encourage them to guess if they are unsure. Explain that spellings do not matter in this exercise.
● Evaluate their findings. Write the answers on the board.
● Sing the song together in French.

## NOW TRY THIS

**1.** Try singing the song again, using Spanish and German.
**2.** Learn another song in English and French, such as 'Frère Jacques'/'Are you sleeping?'
**3.** Call out the animal names in different languages. The children have to respond by making that animal's sounds.

> ### ANSWERS
> French: a dog = *un chien*; a cat = *un chat*; a horse = *un cheval*; a duck = *un canard*; a cow = *une vache*; a pig = *un porc*; a chicken = *un poulet*; a farm = *une ferme*.
> German: a dog = *ein Hund*; a cat = *eine Katze*; a horse = *ein Pferd*; a duck = *eine Ente*; a cow = *eine Kuh*; a pig = *ein Schwein*; a chicken = *ein Huhn*; a farm = *ein Bauernhof*.
> Spanish: a dog = *un perro*; a cat = *un gato*; a horse = *un caballo*; a duck = *un pato*; a cow = *una vaca*; a pig = *un cerdo*; a chicken = *un pollo*; a farm = *una granja*.

# STOP – START

**THINKING SKILL:** reasoning
**SUBJECT LINK:** PE
**LEARNING LINK:** kinaesthetic
**ORGANISATION:** individuals
**RESOURCES:** room with plenty of space for movement (ideally a gym or hall)

## WHAT TO DO

● Tell the children to find a space and listen carefully.
● Their task is to walk or move quickly around the room without bumping into anyone.
● You are going to call out an instruction. They have to carry it out with a specific action. For example, start means walk, fast forward means walk quickly, rewind means walk backwards, pause means to freeze in their position, stop is to stand up straight.
● Call out instructions, speeding up and slowing down as you feel appropriate. Anyone who bumps into someone steps out for one turn and then rejoins.

## NOW TRY THIS

**1.** Try the activity to music.
**2.** When the music stops, call out another instruction.

# WHO AM I?

**THINKING SKILL:** enquiry
**SUBJECT LINK:** history
**ORGANISATION:** whole class
**RESOURCES:** whiteboard and pen

## WHAT TO DO

● Ask one child to leave the room for a short time. The rest of the class then think up who that person is going to be (a historical person).
● When the child comes back in the room, they stand in front of the board. Write the name of the person above their head, so they can't see.
● The child has to ask questions to deduce who they are, for example, *Am I dead? Do I live in Roman times?*
● The rest of the class can only answer *Yes* or *No.*
● Give clues when they are needed. If the person guesses correctly then they can choose who goes outside next.

# WHAT AM I?

**THINKING SKILL:** enquiry, reasoning
**SUBJECT LINK:** literacy
**ORGANISATION:** pairs
**RESOURCES:** pens and paper; 'What am I?' riddles, for example:

1.  I am pink
    I am a bird
    I stand on one leg
    I have three syllables

2.  I contain chips
    I can write letters
    I can add up
    I am a link to the whole wide world

3.  I have hands but I cannot touch
    I can be any shape you want
    I have five letters in me
    I can help you to be punctual

4.  I am see-through
    I am refreshing
    Without me you may die
    I can be hot or cold

## WHAT TO DO

● Tell the children to listen to some riddles and work out what the object is.
● You can repeat the riddles as little or as often as you think appropriate.
● Ask the children to share their answers.
● Ask them to make up their own clues for a friend to work out.

## NOW TRY THIS

Instead of writing the answers to the riddles they could draw the answers.

**ANSWERS**
1. flamingo
2. computer
3. clock
4. water

# DANCE TIME

**THINKING SKILL:** creative thinking
**SUBJECT LINK:** PE
**LEARNING LINK:** kinaesthetic, visual
**ORGANISATION:** pairs
**RESOURCES:** space to move, for example, a gym; different styles of music, for example, 'The Dark Side of the Moon' by Pink Floyd, 'Space March' from 'Themeology' by John Barry, 'The Celtic Harp: A tribute to Edward Bunting' by The Chieftains

## WHAT TO DO

● Let's look at movement. How does a sportsperson move? (Flowing, fast, continuous actions.)
● How about a machine's movements? (They may be jerky, pushing, pulling.) What different kinds of machines can you think of?
● Listen to the music and, in pairs, choose something, like a machine, or a spinning top. Think about how it moves.
● Work together to move around your partner, going in circles, meeting, parting, pushing, pulling.
● Think about the top part of your body, then your middle, then the lower part.

## NOW TRY THIS

With your partner, slow down your actions and then speed them up.

# RAPPING RHYTHM

**THINKING SKILL:** creative thinking
**SUBJECT LINK:** music
**LEARNING LINK:** kinaesthetic
**ORGANISATION:** large groups
**RESOURCES:** none required

## WHAT TO DO

● Ask the children whether they know what a rhythm is. Give an example by clapping your hands together: two quick claps, pause, and then two slow claps.

● Tell the children to build on this rhythm by adding more sounds.
● Split them into two groups, each sitting in a circle. Elect one person in each group to go first. That person will be 'A'. 'A' starts the rhythm, then each child repeats the sequence adding one sound of their own until everyone has had a turn in continuing the rapping rhythm.
● Try it with the children making other sounds such as *shh*, *tippity tap*, *phut*, *boing*. Tell them to use any part of their bodies, including voices, to extend and keep the rhythm going without too many pauses.
● When the rhythm gets back to 'A', all the children in the circle do the final rhythm together.

## NOW TRY THIS

Once the class has a rhythm going, encourage some children to add a rap over the top of it.

# TRUE OR FALSE

**THINKING SKILL:** information processing
**SUBJECT LINK:** art
**ORGANISATION:** individuals
**RESOURCES:** pen and paper; examples of direct statements (the following are all art-related):

> *Artists are always right-handed.*
> *David Hockney is from Holland.*
> *Monet and Manet are the same person.*
> *George Stubbs painted horses.*
> *Salvador Dali was bald.*
> *Foot painting is impossible.*
> *Michelaneglo did a sculpture called 'David'.*

## WHAT TO DO

● This is the true or false game. All you have to do is listen to the statements and write *True* or *False* on your paper.
● Now compare your answers with a partner.

## NOW TRY THIS

Make up your own true and false game to try out on your friends.

### ANSWERS
False
False – David Hockney is from the UK.
False – both were French Impressionist artists.
True
False – Dali had long hair in a ponytail.
False
True

# WAVY FACTS

**THINKING SKILL:** evaluation
**SUBJECT LINK:** RE
**LEARNING LINK:** kinaesthetic
**ORGANISATION:** individuals
**RESOURCES:** sample statements (adapt/create for your class):

1. *All Christians go to church.*
2. *Religious people are always good people.*
3. *Buddha lived in the 20th century.*
4. *Christmas is a Christian festival.*
5. *There are 3 pillars of Islam.*
6. *Buddhists don't believe in God.*
7. *Hindus worship in a temple.*
8. *Lent lasts for a week.*
9. *Muslims believe in one God.*
10. *In the Bible there are 7 commandments.*
11. *Baptised Sikhs carry a small sword.*
12. *The Jewish special book is called the Torah.*

## WHAT TO DO

● Explain that you are going to read out some statements. Each one is true or false.
● If they think it's true, they wave their arms in the air.
● If they think it's false, they keep their hands in their laps.
● If they aren't sure, they put their arms out straight and move their hands (the 'so-so' sign).
● Explain that it doesn't matter what other people do – this is about what they think.
● If they are the only person who thinks it's true – that's fine.
● Ask for explanations, for example, *Why do you think it's false?*
● Some of these statements and responses could generate questions, curiosity and challenges. Provide follow up/research time.

### ANSWERS
1. False. 2. False. 3. False – Buddha lived between *c.*563BC and *c.*483BC. 4. True. 5. False, there are five pillars of Islam. 6. True. 7. True. 8. False – Lent lasts for 40 days. 9. True. 10. False – there are ten commandments. 11. True – baptised Sikhs carry a small sword called a Kirpan, an emblem of power and courage. 12. True.

# SING-A-LONG A SONG

**THINKING SKILL:** creative thinking
**SUBJECT LINK:** music
**ORGANISATION:** groups of three or four
**RESOURCES:** 'Ten green bottles' counting song

## WHAT TO DO

● Tell the children they are going to make up a singing game in their groups. It could be a counting song, a tongue twister, a clapping game, or an action song.
● Explain that the song needs to have a strong beat and a catchy rhythm and should be four lines long. They should think about using repetition rhyme.
● Sing 'Ten green bottles' as a class and use it as a starting point together with any other songs they suggest.
● The groups use the class song, or one of their own choice. They could use 'Ten green bottles' as a template, inventing ideas such as seven wise owls, twelve muddy shoes, and so on.

## NOW TRY THIS
The song could be linked to various themes such as pollution, poverty or famine. Encourage a performance of all the pieces.

# PICTURE PAINTING

**THINKING SKILL:** enquiry, reasoning, creative thinking
**SUBJECT LINK:** art
**LEARNING LINK:** visual
**ORGANISATION:** individuals
**RESOURCES:** for each child: a paint palette, a water pot and a paintbrush; painting overalls; a picture book story

## WHAT TO DO

● Tell the children that you are going to read them a story. As they listen they are going to paint a picture. They can paint a picture of something that happens in the story, a character, a landscape, or something inspired by the story.

● They can put up their hands if they want to ask a question to do with the story or with their painting, such as *How do I paint a big sky?* and ask the other children for suggestions.

● Encourage the children to help each other and to find their own solutions for interpreting the words and painting a picture.

● Compare the paintings.

## NOW TRY THIS

Instead of listening to a story, the children can listen to different styles of music and draw a picture or pattern inspired by it.

# IT'S DARK IN HERE

**THINKING SKILL:** creative thinking
**SUBJECT LINK:** literacy
**ORGANISATION:** groups of three or four
**RESOURCES:** pen and paper for each group: the poem 'It's Dark in Here' by Shel Silverstein from *Where the Sidewalk Ends* (HarperCollins)

## WHAT TO DO

● Read the poem aloud starting quietly, getting louder and then softer towards the end.

● Ask the children to think of some dark places. Where are they and why are they dark?

● Write their responses on the board in the form of a mind map.

● Ask them if they like dark places and what these places mean to them. Are they comforting or scary?

● Read the poem several times quietly. Give the children time to think. Ask them to write down as many dark places as they can think of.

## NOW TRY THIS

**1.** Encourage the children to focus on one 'dark place' or image from the list and use it as the starting point for a poem.
**2.** Ask the children to imagine a magic object is hidden in their dark place. What does it look like and what powers does it have?

# TREASURE BOX

**THINKING SKILL:** enquiry, evaluation, reasoning
**SUBJECT LINK:** general
**LEARNING LINK:** visual
**ORGANISATION:** whole class, pairs
**RESOURCES:** pencils and paper; a copy of the poem 'The Magic Box' by Kit Wright from *Cat Among The Pigeons* (Puffin Books); a list of questions on the board:

*What is a treasure box?*
*Do you have one special treasure?*
*Do you own something you love yet has no value at all?*
*What is the most precious thing in the world?*
*If you found some treasure, who would it belong to?*
*What sort of treasure is found in a fairy tale?*
*If you had three wishes, what would you wish for?*
*Are you someone's 'treasure'?*
*If you had a treasure box, what colour would it be?*
*Do wishes come true?*

## WHAT TO DO

● Read the poem to the class and discuss what the children would put into a magic box.

● Ask them to sort and order the ten questions against set criteria, for example:
  ● Select your top three questions.
  ● Select the three questions you'd least like to answer.
  ● Order the questions putting those you'd most like to answer first, followed by those you'd least like to.
  ● Which is the best/worst question?
  ● Which questions, when answered, give you the most/least useful information?
  ● Which question is easiest/hardest to answer. Why?

## NOW TRY THIS

Ask the children to answer with another question. For example: Question: *Are you someone's treasure?* Answer: *If I am, how would I know?*

# I SAY, YOU SAY

**THINKING SKILL:** enquiry
**SUBJECT LINK:** literacy – speaking and listening
**ORGANISATION:** pairs
**RESOURCES:** pen and paper; a list of sounds to say to the class, for example:

| I SAY | YOU SAY (examples) |
|-------|--------------------|
| ee | eel |
| oo | fool |
| ae | say |
| sh | shop |
| th | think |
| br | break |
| ph | telephone |
| tr | treasure |
| igh | lightning |
| ur | learning |

## WHAT TO DO

● Tell the children you have found a machine that swallows words and spits out any it does not like the look of. It only spits out part of the word.

● Take the word *feel*. The machine swallows the word whole but spits out *ee*. They need to make these words whole again by adding letters at the beginning or end of the sound (or at the beginning and end) and write them down.

● Say the sounds from the grid slowly with pauses in between. Give the children time to write down a complete word. The spellings do not matter as this is a listening game.

## NOW TRY THIS

**1.** Ask the children to make up their own machine that spits out parts of words, for example, *oo* sounds. How many words can they think up that contain the sound *oo*?

**2.** They can do this for any sounds and write words from any language.

# TIME MACHINE

**THINKING SKILL:** enquiry, creative thinking
**SUBJECT LINK:** history, literacy, art, design and technology
**LEARNING LINK:** visual
**ORGANISATION:** individuals, pairs
**RESOURCES:** A copy of 'Rip Van Winkle' by Robert Fisher, adapted from a story by Washington Irving, from *Stories for Thinking* (Nash Pollock Publishing); paper and felt-tipped pens; a list of questions addressed to the children while they draw, for example:

*What material is your time machine made from?*
*Who would you take with you?*
*How big is it?*
*What colour is it?*
*How do you enter the machine?*
*How do you exit the machine?*
*Has it got special features?*
*What supplies would you take with you?*
*How does it move – fly, motor, swim?*
*What kind of fuel does it need?*

## WHAT TO DO

● Listen to the story your teacher reads. Discuss what it would feel like to wake-up and find that everything had changed. Talk about any stories that use time machines, such as *Doctor Who*.

● Imagine you have a time machine and can travel anywhere, back or forward in time.

● In pairs, talk about where you would go in time. If you go back in time, is there anything you would like to change?

● Draw a picture of your time machine.

## NOW TRY THIS

If your time machine took you backwards or forwards in time by only 60 seconds, what could you do to help people?

# CATCH ME IF YOU CAN

**THINKING SKILL:** reasoning
**SUBJECT LINK:** PE, drama
**LEARNING LINK:** kinaesthetic
**ORGANISATION:** pairs
**RESOURCES:** a large space; blindfolds for everyone

## WHAT TO DO

● Ask pairs to choose who is 'A' and who is 'B'.

● Each pair is given the name of an animal and the sound it makes, for example, a donkey – eeaw.

● Each child stands at the opposite end of the space from their partner. Ask them to put on their blindfolds. Each child spins round five times.

● Tell them to make their animal sounds until they find their partner by listening for their sound and moving towards them.

## NOW TRY THIS

When they are confident, each pair can be given different animal sounds. They have to find their partner by following their partner's sound.

# HUMAN HARMONY

**THINKING SKILL:** evaluation
**SUBJECT LINK:** music
**LEARNING LINK:** kinaesthetic
**ORGANISATION:** two groups
**RESOURCES:** the words doh, ray, me, fah, soh, lah, te, doh written on the board; a recording of *The Sound of Music* by Rogers and Hammerstein; a xylophone

## WHAT TO DO

● Ask the children if they have seen *The Sound of Music* and play 'Do-ray-me'. Play middle C on the xylophone and go up the scale. Ask group one to sing up and down the scale starting at middle C with doh, ray, me, and so on and carry on up the scale.

● Group two sings the note doh, and holds it. Now swap and change the doh-ray-me sound to oo-oe-ch. The other group holds the first sound (oo) as long as possible. Compare the different sounds and what works well.

## NOW TRY THIS

**1.** Start a round with both groups singing at the same time, but from different starting points.

**2.** Vary the tempo and the dynamics, raising your hand up and down to show when to sing softly and when louder.

**3.** Record these harmonies and play back for evaluation.

# HISTORY MAKER

**THINKING SKILL:** creative thinking
**SUBJECT LINK:** history
**LEARNING LINK:** visual
**ORGANISATION:** pairs
**RESOURCES:** a selection of history vocabulary and phrases written on the board, for example, Sir Winston Churchill, First man on the moon, Queen Elizabeth II crowned, Titanic hits an iceberg and sinks, Roman soldier

## WHAT TO DO

● Ask the children to read the words. Ask them to write down as many other words as they can linked to any period of history.

● Tell the children they are going to invent a new piece of history and you are going to tell them a story and you want them to finish it.

> *Sir Winston Churchill was sitting with his feet up reading the newspaper when suddenly he heard a huge BANG at the front of the ship! He had seen some Roman soldiers marching up and down on deck for the last 30 minutes and there were some men hiding behind one of the lifeboats with guns under their coats. Was it something to do with those soldiers or something more sinister? The* Titanic *was on its maiden voyage and Mr Churchill felt rather cross that his afternoon had been interrupted. What happened next?*

● Ask the children to carry on the story, making it up in pairs.

## NOW TRY THIS

**1.** Ask the children what they found easy and what was more challenging. Ask them to tell their stories to the class.

**2.** They could write down their stories as part of an alternative history lesson.

# JOURNEY OF LIFE

**THINKING SKILL:** enquiry
**SUBJECT LINK:** general
**LEARNING LINK:** visual
**ORGANISATION:** individuals
**RESOURCES:** felt-tipped pens; paper; recording of gentle rock (such as 'Freebird' by Lynyrd Skynyrd) or classical music

## WHAT TO DO

● There are thoughts in your brain wandering around trying to find the way out. We have lots of thoughts, but they often don't really have any shape.

● Relax, listen to music, and draw a thought – this means that some thoughts have a chance to get out and be free.

● It doesn't have to be a proper picture; it can be a pattern of colours, a happy thought, confused thought, or silly thought.

● Draw the pictures these thoughts create or write down what you see and feel.

# WHICH WORD?

**THINKING SKILL:** evaluation
**SUBJECT LINK:** modern languages
**LEARNING LINK:** visual
**ORGANISATION:** pairs
**RESOURCES:** pens and paper; the following words written on the board:

> 1. *bene, bon, good, bad, gut, buon*
> 2. *goodbye, au revoir, chat, arrividerci*
> 3. *ola, hi, ciao, salut, table*
> 4. *noir, non, ne, no, nein*

## WHAT TO DO

● Say each of the words in the lists, one set at a time.

● Get the children to repeat each word. Can they recognise any or guess what they mean?

● All but one word in each set means the same thing but in another language.

● Ask them to find the odd one out and write it down.

● They compare findings with another pair.

## NOW TRY THIS

**1.** Complete the set by replacing the odd one out with the same word in another language.

**2.** Which words sound the most similar? Is there a pattern in words that sound similar in different languages?

***

**ANSWERS**

1. bad   2. chat   3. table   4. noir
Children may give other valid solutions.

***

# ARTISTIC THINKING HATS

**THINKING SKILL:** enquiry
**SUBJECT LINK:** art
**LEARNING LINK:** visual
**ORGANISATION:** individuals
**RESOURCES:** a variety of hats for dressing up; pencils; A3 paper

## WHAT TO DO

● Ask the children to choose a thinking hat and put it on. When they wear the hat, it gives them special powers so they can draw anything without thinking too hard.

● When you call out a word or phrase they draw a quick sketch of the first thing that comes into their mind.

● Call out a general object, such as *seat* or *something to sit on* that could be interpreted as a stool, an armchair, a sofa, a bed, a school chair, a throne, or a bench. The children can think of the objects around them, or they can be fanciful, perhaps drawing their ideal chair. Other examples are something to lie on, a fun place to go, a scary place.

● Ask them to compare drawing with and without the hats. Which things are easiest to draw. Why?

## NOW TRY THIS

**1.** Ask the children to think up some more objects to sit on and what type of place each one has been designed for, such as a palace, classroom, church, playground.

**2.** Give them a theme for drawing, for example, all the things have to be in a palace, and then ask them to draw something to sit on, something to eat, and so on.

# ALL ABOARD!

**THINKING SKILL:** information processing, reasoning
**SUBJECT LINK:** PE, Drama
**LEARNING LINK:** kinaesthetic
**ORGANISATION:** groups of three or four
**RESOURCES:** space to sit on the floor; various sailing instructions to read aloud to the children during the 'sailing trip', written on the board, for example:

---

*Hoist the sails – put up the sails*
*Lee ho – turning*
*Tacking – turn right*
*Jibbing – turn left*
*Ahoy! – hello to pirates!*
*Port – the left side of a boat looking forward*
*Starboard – the right side of a boat looking forward*

---

## WHAT TO DO

● Sit in a line, as if you were in a long rowing boat.

● Imagine you are sailing in a race across the English Channel, starting at Cowes on the Isle of Wight and finishing in Cherbourg, France.

● In your boats, decide who is captain, who is first mate and who is navigator.

● Your teacher will call out instructions.

● The captains pass on commands to the first mates, who in turn pass them on to the navigators.

● For example, your teacher might say *Storm blowing in the east; Hoist the sails*. All the captains repeat this to the first mates, who repeat it to the navigators. Everyone has to act out hoisting the sails.

## NOW TRY THIS

Try it with the captains making up their own instructions and the sailors in the boats moving with the instructions and leaning the appropriate ways.

# NEGATIVES TO POSITIVES

**THINKING SKILL:** information processing, evaluation
**SUBJECT LINK:** literacy
**ORGANISATION:** pairs
**RESOURCES:** copies of the following statements, one for each pair, as examples:

| | |
|---|---|
| 1. I can't do joined up handwriting. | You write your letters really neatly. |
| 2. I can't write long stories. | You tell stories that are imaginative and exciting. |
| 3. I can't draw. | You colour in beautifully. |
| 4. I can't swim. | You're brave and can put your face under water. |
| 5. I can't skip. | You can hop really fast. |
| 6. I am a real fidget. | You can sit still for a whole lesson now. |
| 7. I am useless at spelling. | You write really creative poetry. |
| 8. I am not very good at reading. | You have made good progress reading this term. |
| 9. I am a slow runner. | You're a great goalie in football. |
| 10. I am shy around large groups of people. | You're great speaking one to one. |

## WHAT TO DO

● Do you often make negative statements about yourself? For example, *I can't do division.*

● Say one thing that is negative about yourself to your partner.

● Your partner should say a linked positive statement back, for example, *You are very good at adding sums.*

● Your teacher will say ten different negative statements. With your partner, think up positive statements as a response.

● Say your responses aloud. Write them down if you want to.

# QUICK FIRE QUESTIONS

**THINKING SKILL:** enquiry, reasoning, creative thinking
**SUBJECT LINK:** general
**ORGANISATION:** individuals, pairs
**RESOURCES:** a selection of dressing up hats; a list of problems, for example:

> *There's a toad in the bed.*
> *There's an alien at the door.*
> *The cat's been sick.*
> *All your clothes are dirty.*
> *Your mum's on strike.*
> *The bath's overflowing.*
> *The fridge is empty.*
> *There's a big spot on your nose.*
> *It's hot outside and you've only got a winter coat to wear.*
> *There's a mouse in the cupboard.*

## WHAT TO DO

● Ask the children to choose a hat and put it on. Explain that it will help them sort out problems.
● Ask them to tell a problem to a friend and then swap roles. Each time, the other person has to give a quick response, however silly.
● Read out the problems from the list. Tell the children to say to their partners the first thing that comes into their heads to sort out the problem.
● Ask the children to come up with a list of problems. These can be silly or sensible.

## NOW TRY THIS

Introduce some real life problems: global warming, the ozone layer, more cars on the road. Ask them to discuss their suggestions.

# WHERE IN THE WORLD HAVE YOU BEEN?

**THINKING SKILL:** information processing
**SUBJECT LINK:** geography
**ORGANISATION:** small groups, whole class
**RESOURCES:** one sheet of A3 paper; marker pens; globes or maps of the world

## WHAT TO DO

● Have you ever visited another part of the world?
● Can you find it on the map?

● When you have found it, explain to the group what the country was like – weather, landmarks, food, language, people.
● One group member writes down where everyone went and three things about the country.
● Make sure everyone has a chance to speak – even if they haven't been to another country.
● When you have all had a turn, choose a country and put a circle round it.
● Now give the class the three clues to your chosen country.
● For example, if someone has been to France, they could say, *The country I have visited is in Europe. You can travel to it by car and ferry, plane or by the Euro tunnel. I ate baguettes for breakfast and learned how to say 'Bonjour'.*

# RHYTHMIC RAP

**THINKING SKILL:** creative thinking
**SUBJECT LINK:** literacy, drama
**LEARNING LINK:** kinaesthetic
**ORGANISATION:** groups of three or four
**RESOURCES:** A recording by Bob Marley and the Wailers; a variety of short poems such as 'It's Dark in Here' by Shel Silverstein in *Where the Sidewalk Ends* (HarperCollins), 'Friends' in *Poems for Circle Time and Literacy Hour* by Margaret Goldthorpe (LDA)

## WHAT TO DO

● Tell the groups to elect one child to collect a poem.
● Listen to the music together. Tell them that it is African–Caribbean music with a strong beat.
● Get the children to copy the beat by clapping, tapping, or clicking their fingers.
● They familiarise themselves with the poem, imagine it has a rap beat and perform it as a 'rhythmic rap'.
● Tell them to decide among themselves who performs which lines and what sort of beat and rhythm they need.
● Encourage the children to clap, tap, or click fingers to keep the beat going.
● They have five minutes to practise before they perform their poem.

# FAST OPERATION

**THINKING SKILL:** information processing
**SUBJECT LINK:** mathematics
**ORGANISATION:** pairs
**RESOURCES:** a number operation matched to your learners' abilities, for example: multiply by three; ten numbers to which the operation can be applied, for example: multiply by three can be applied to 10, 11, 12, 13, 14, 15, 16, 17, 18, 19 (write the operation and the ten numbers on the board)

## WHAT TO DO

● Decide who is 'A' and who is 'B'.
● Sit so that you are facing each other, but only 'A' can see the board.
● 'A' says the numbers one at a time in any order.
● 'B' has to apply the number operation as fast as they can to each number.
● Swap seats so that 'A' can't see the numbers but 'B' can.
● 'B' says the numbers and 'A' has to do the number operation.
● Talk about which ones were harder. Did you always find the same answers?

# THE HUMAN EMAIL

**THINKING SKILL:** information processing
**SUBJECT LINK:** ICT
**LEARNING LINK:** kinaesthetic
**ORGANISATION:** whole class
**RESOURCES:** text to read out:

> *Jade wanted to organise a sleepover so she decided to email her friends. She turned on the computer and started to create her invitations. While she was typing, an email from her brother Ben arrived so she decided to reply. She also thought her friend Carly would like to read Ben's email, so she hit 'forward'. Just then, Mum called her for tea so she had to save her invitation for later.*

## WHAT TO DO

● Tell the children that they are going to learn about emailing – without a computer!
● Explain that you can create an email, save it, send it and forward it. You can also reply to email that people send you. You can send email to more than one person at once – like sending one letter that arrives through lots of letterboxes.

● Explain that they are going to learn actions for the things you can do with email:
  ● Email (draw the @ sign in the air)
  ● Create (wiggle all your fingers as if typing)
  ● Save (put a letter in a drawer)
  ● Send (put a letter in a post box)
  ● Forward (bring your right hand towards your mouth like you're calling someone over, then push the same hand away from you)
  ● Reply (bring your right hand towards you and push away with your left).
● Say the actions above as the children practise the movements.
● Read the above extract about email, extend and elaborate as necessary. The children listen. Every time they hear one of the email words, they do the action.

# WHAT'S THAT NOISE?

**THINKING SKILL:** enquiry
**SUBJECT LINK:** music
**ORGANISATION:** pairs
**RESOURCES:** pen and paper for each pair; write on the board an example of something that makes sounds, and words to describes the sounds, for example, *running water – whooshing, splashing, trickling*

## WHAT TO DO

● Look at the board. Discuss what running water sounds like.
● How many other describing words can you think of to describe it?
● Go outside and listen to the sounds around you. What can you hear?
● Think about children moving around in the corridors. What sounds do they make?
● Back in the classroom, listen to the noises around you. What words would you use to describe them, for instance – paper being screwed up and thrown in the bin sounds scrunched and scratchy.
● Write down as many words as you can to describe the sounds you hear.

## NOW TRY THIS

Say a sound to your partner. They write down the words to describe that sound. Swap, and you do the writing.

# CREATE-A-PLACE

**THINKING SKILL:** creative thinking
**SUBJECT LINK:** geography
**LEARNING LINK:** visual
**ORGANISATION:** whole class
**RESOURCES:** a sound effects recording that includes sounds linked to places or travel (for example, running water, a plane taking off, thunder, a car screeching to a halt); paper; pens

## WHAT TO DO

• You can hear different sounds in different places. Sometimes it's possible to tell where you are by the sounds.
• Close your eyes. Listen to the sound effect your teacher is playing.
• Where might you hear that sound?
• Write down three words or draw something about this place.
• Share your thoughts with a partner.
• Listen to more sound effects your teacher plays. What do they make you think of?

## NOW TRY THIS

**1.** Write down three different words, each linked to a place.
**2.** What sound effects would you need to describe your words?

# THOUGHT BELLS

**THINKING SKILL:** creative thinking
**SUBJECT LINK:** RE, PSHE
**LEARNING LINK:** visual
**ORGANISATION:** whole class
**RESOURCES:** one or more percussion instruments – tuned and untuned, for example, a hand bell, a drum, cymbals, shakers; coloured pens/pencils and paper

## WHAT TO DO

• Explain that some religions use simple sounds in worship, prayer and meditation. The sounds can tell people what part of the worship they have reached or 'clear the air' when people are praying or meditating.
• Make some sounds with a percussion instrument. Ask the children what pictures and colours come into their heads when they hear it.
• The children use coloured pens to draw or write down what their mind creates when they hear the sound. Give them a few minutes.
• Ring, hit or play other percussion instruments. Give two minutes of response time. Repeat with other instruments.

## NOW TRY THIS

Ask the children to start by drawing a coloured picture. They then decide which percussion instrument it's most like. They could invent a new instrument!

# ICT PAIRS

**THINKING SKILL:** evaluation
**SUBJECT LINK:** ICT
**ORGANISATION:** pairs
**RESOURCES:** a list of ICT equipment and each one's predecessor (alternatively – have real examples or pictures):

| Digital camera | Camera with film |
|---|---|
| Wordprocessor | Typewriter |
| Video camera | Cine camera |
| Mobile phone | Normal home phone |
| iPod | Personal stereo (tape or CD) |
| Television | Radio |
| DVD | Video |
| Hand-held computer game | Board game |
| Interactive whiteboard | White/Blackboard |

## WHAT TO DO

• One person is a modern piece of ICT equipment, like a mobile phone, the other person is the traditional equivalent, like a normal house phone.
• You have one minute to think up why you're better than your partner.
• Write down your thoughts if you want to.
• You've got one minute to tell each other why you're better, 30 seconds each.
• Say things like, *I'm a mobile phone, and I'm better than you because...*
• Choose other ICT pairs.

## WHAT IS YOUR PROBLEM?

**THINKING SKILL:** creative thinking
**SUBJECT LINK:** mathematics
**ORGANISATION:** small groups
**RESOURCES:** one appropriate mathematical sentence per group, for example: 15 x 4 + 12, 70 + 29 – 14, 5 x 3 – 10, 10 + 10 – 15; one whiteboard and pen (or paper and pencil) per group

### WHAT TO DO

● Your teacher will give each group a different mathematical sentence.
● You need to design a mathematical problem/story around this sentence. For example, if your sentence says 25 x 4 – 15, a suitable story/problem could be: A farmer had four fields. In each field he had 25 cows. One windy morning the fence in one field blew down. Fifteen cows escaped. How many cows does the farmer have now?
● Your group needs to know the answer to the problem before you have finished.
● Once you have written your problem down, you can read it to another group. Can they solve it?
● You will be given a problem to solve by another group. Can you solve it?

## AUDIO TALLY

**THINKING SKILL:** information processing
**LEARNING LINK:** visual
**SUBJECT LINK:** general
**ORGANISATION:** individual
**RESOURCES:** paper; pens/pencils; extract of an audio recording (few minutes) – fiction or non-fiction; selection of key words and/or phrases which appear in the recording written on the board

### WHAT TO DO

● Copy the key words on to your paper.
● You're going to listen to a short recording that contains all of these words. Put a circle around the word you think will be most used.
● Listen carefully to the recording. Every time you hear one of the key words or phrases from your sheet, put a tally mark under it.
● When the recording is stopped, count up how many of each word you heard.
● Which word was most used? Was your guess correct?
● Compare your answers with a partner.

## IDEA MAP

**THINKING SKILL:** reasoning
**SUBJECT LINK:** design and technology
**LEARNING LINK:** visual
**ORGANISATION:** pairs
**RESOURCES:** concept map:

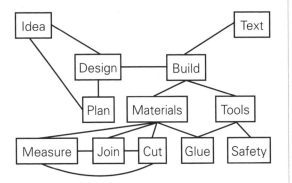

### WHAT TO DO

● Draw the above map of ideas.
● If there is a line joining two ideas, it means they are linked. For example:
    *'Design' is joined to 'Build' because a design makes you think about what you're going to build before you start.*
    *'Materials' is joined to 'Measure' because you have to measure how much you want.*
● Describe the ideas links clearly, like in the examples – remember to use the word *because*.
● If you describe all the links, add more of your own.

### NOW TRY THIS

Create other ideas maps. Think of a subject, close your eyes and say the first ten words you can think of on the subject. Your partner writes them down. Work together to describe the links.

# FIND YOUR BODY PART

**THINKING SKILL:** information processing
**SUBJECT LINK:** science
**LEARNING LINK:** kinaesthetic, visual
**ORGANISATION:** whole class
**RESOURCES:** A5 sheets with body parts written on; an example of some body part matches: thigh and upper leg, calf and lower leg, spine and back; safety pin/masking tape

## WHAT TO DO
● Your teacher will stick a piece of paper on to your back. You cannot see it!
● This piece of paper will have a body part written on it.
● When everyone has their papers attached, stand up and find space in the room.
● Your job is to find the person who has the body part that matches yours.
● For example, one person may have spine and one person may have back – they are matches and need to pair up.
● You will need to ask questions and help others.
● The rules are: you cannot ask anyone directly what is written on your back; you cannot tell anyone directly what is written on theirs.
● The exercise is complete when everybody has found a match.

## NOW TRY THIS
Use different types of matches – authors and books, capital cities and countries.

# EAR PATTERNS

**THINKING SKILL:** reasoning
**SUBJECT LINK:** mathematics
**ORGANISATION:** pairs
**RESOURCES:** none required

## WHAT TO DO
● You can make only three types of sound: clicking fingers, Shhhh and Ha.
● Invent a pattern with four of these sounds, for example: click, click, Shhhh, Ha.
● Make the pattern twice to your partner, who listens carefully.
● Your partner has to copy your pattern back to you twice.
● Swap so that your partner makes another pattern. Listen and copy it.

## NOW TRY THIS
**1.** With the same three sounds, challenge yourselves by making patterns of five or six sounds and/or closing your eyes while listening.
**2.** Decrease or increase the number of sounds that can make the pattern.

# WHY OH WHY?

**THINKING SKILL:** enquiry
**SUBJECT LINK:** RE, PSHE
**ORGANISATION:** whole class
**RESOURCES:** the following statements or similar:

*People should not steal.*
*Some people believe in God.*
*It's right to help others.*
*Some people argue about what's right and what's wrong.*
*It's good to think for yourself.*
*You must respect other people's beliefs.*
*People act differently when they're with their friends.*

## WHAT TO DO
● Tell the class that children are good at finding things out because they are not scared to ask questions, especially *Why?*
● Ask for a volunteer to take the *Why?* challenge.
● Read out a statement. The rest of the class has to say *Why?* – all together.
● The volunteer must try to answer starting with the word *Because...*
● Then the class replies with *Why?*
● Then there's another *Because*, and so on.
● The challenge is to answer the greatest number of *Why* questions with *Because* replies that make sense.
● When the volunteer has had enough they say, *No more whys* and the class say *Well done!*

## NOW TRY THIS
Replace *Why?/Because...* with *So what?/I'll tell you what...*

# CREATIVE CODING

**THINKING SKILL:** creative thinking
**SUBJECT LINK:** ICT
**LEARNING LINK:** visual
**ORGANISATION:** class
**RESOURCES:** a mobile phone (optional); two A3 sheets stuck to the wall or board for the class to see and write on, one with the alphabet already written on; pens

## WHAT TO DO

● Ask the children to put up their hands if they use mobile phones.
● What style of texting do they use?
● Why do they text? How often? Who do they text?
● Do they use abbreviations? If they do, they can come up and write an abbreviated word on the A3 sheet.
● Ask the class to work out what the word means. Write the meaning on the board.
● Some things are visual, like smileys, but some abbreviated words rely on sounding like (but not looking like) the original.
● Write *C U L8tr*. It doesn't make sense, but it does if you say it out loud. Ask the class to translate the phrase. (*See you later.*)
● Ask them to think of a new way of abbreviating a word or a phrase. They may already be using unique abbreviations.
● Give them a minute to look at the A3 alphabet sheet and think.
● When they have an idea, they write the word on the plain sheet. Can the class work out what it says?

# SPOT THE DIFFERENCE

**THINKING SKILL:** evaluation
**SUBJECT LINK:** science
**LEARNING LINK:** visual
**ORGANISATION:** pairs, whole class
**RESOURCES:** pencils; paper; two different electrical circuits, one must include a light bulb and the other three light bulbs – all bulbs lit

## WHAT TO DO

● Look closely at these two electrical circuits.
● Can you spot the differences?
● Write down or draw the differences.

● Now think: which circuit is the best and why?
● Share your thinking with a partner. Convey your ideas clearly. You need to listen to your partner because your teacher may ask you to share what they said with the class.

# MY FAVOURITE PLACES

**THINKING SKILL:** evaluation
**SUBJECT LINK:** geography
**LEARNING LINK:** visual
**ORGANISATION:** individuals, pairs
**RESOURCES:** pens/pencils; paper; a list of five different places, written on the board – for example:

> *By a river, in a forest, on top of a mountain, in a garden, in a cave*
> *In the park, at the swimming pool, in a restaurant, at the cinema, in a shop*
> *Five places in the locality familiar to the children*
> *Five places studied in class familiar to the children*

## WHAT TO DO

● Let's read these five places out loud.
● Listen to these instructions:
  ● Draw a vertical line on your paper.
  ● At the top of the line, write down the place you'd most like to be.
  ● At the bottom of the line, write down the place you'd least like to be.
  ● Write the other three places on the line to show how much you'd like to be there.
  ● Compare your line to your partner's.
  ● Discuss any differences.

## NOW TRY THIS

Play the game with historical figures. Make a list of historical people. Write down who you would most like to be at the top. Order the rest with the person you would least like to be at the bottom.

## MATHS WHISPERS

**THINKING SKILL:** enquiry
**SUBJECT LINK:** mathematics
**ORGANISATION:** groups of four to eight, sitting in a semi-circle
**RESOURCES:** copies of target multiplication tables/ number facts

### WHAT TO DO

● Choose a multiplication table that your group wants to work on.
● Choose the 'First Whisperer' (this person has a copy of the table, which they keep hidden).
● The First Whisperer chooses a question, and its answer, and whispers both to the next person, for example, *6 times 7 is 42*.

● That person listens carefully and passes the whisper on to their neighbour, who does the same. It can only be whispered once for each person.
● When the whisper gets back to the First Whisperer, they reveal the original question and answer.
● The First Whisperer then asks three questions:
   ● Did any thing change on the way round?
   ● If so, what? If not, what made us do it well?
   ● Who thinks they now know this number fact?

## HOW HEALTHY IS MY CLASS?

**THINKING SKILL:** information processing
**SUBJECT LINK:** PSHE, RE
**ORGANISATION:** groups of around five
**RESOURCES:** none required

### WHAT TO DO

● You have five minutes to collect as many facts as you can about how the members of your group lead healthy lives.
● You get one point for each different fact.
● Take it in turns to speak – you need to listen carefully to what each person says.
● Try to get more than five points.

● Now choose one word for each fact. Get ready to share these with the class.
● For example, if someone swims twice a week, the word could be swimming.

## IT TAKES A FRACTION OF TIME

**THINKING SKILL:** enquiry
**SUBJECT LINK:** mathematics
**ORGANISATION:** whole class
**RESOURCES:** an area for the class to sit down together

### WHAT TO DO

● Sit the children down together in a circle.
● Choose one child. Whisper a simple fraction in his or her ear, for example, say *one third* or *two quarters*.
● The rest of the class shouldn't hear what you say.
● The chosen person returns to the circle.
● The class has to find out what the fraction is.
● Encourage them to think up clever questions, for example, *Do you have a higher value than one half?* or *Is your numerator more than one?*
● Once they have discovered what the fraction is, choose somebody else and repeat the process.

## GO HOME!

**THINKING SKILL:** information processing
**SUBJECT LINK:** geography
**LEARNING LINK:** visual
**ORGANISATION:** pairs
**RESOURCES:** paper; pencils

### WHAT TO DO

● Imagine that you are giving directions to your house to a friend, by drawing a map.
● This is not as easy as it sounds because of two rules:
   ● You can talk but not point or draw (sit on your hands!)
   ● Your partner can only draw but not speak.
● Describe the route. Tell them how to draw the map. Use instructions like, *Draw a road going up with a roundabout at the top.*

# THE MUG OF LEARNING

**THINKING SKILL:** creative thinking
**SUBJECT LINK:** design and technology
**LEARNING LINK:** visual
**ORGANISATION:** small groups
**RESOURCES:** A3 paper; marker pens; a selection of real mugs

## WHAT TO DO

- Your group will design a learning mug.
- The special thing about the mug is that it's a talking mug and it says different things. Every time you tip it up to take a sip, it says something different.
- It could ask questions like *Spell 'night'* or *What's 5 times 7?* or *What are you thinking about?* Or it could remind you of facts: *World War II started in 1939.* Or it could motivate you: *Well done, you're a great thinker!*
- You'll take ten sips from the mug, so think up ten different things for it to say. Write them down.
- Will you make each thing it says different or repeat certain things?

## NOW TRY THIS

Design a learning mug for a specific subject.

# TELL ME THE SECRET!

**THINKING SKILL:** information processing
**SUBJECT LINK:** mathematics
**LEARNING LINK:** kinaesthetic
**ORGANISATION:** groups of three
**RESOURCES:** identical objects built from Multilink™ (or similar) cubes – to be placed in an area outside the classroom (enough for a third of your class to easily look at one of them. The shapes should match the children's ability); an adequate supply of cubes for each group to duplicate the object

## WHAT TO DO

- There are secret objects in the next room/outside and your team ('A',' B' and 'C') is going to build a copy. Each object is the same, so it doesn't matter which one you look at.

- There are some rules:
  - 'A' is the looker and talker – allowed to look at the secret object and describe it to 'B'.
  - 'B' is the instructor – allowed to listen to 'A' and talk to 'C', but can't ask questions.
  - 'C' is the builder – allowed to build and listen to 'B'. 'C' cannot talk.
  - 'A' must not communicate with 'C' at all.
  - 'A' has one minute to examine the object.
  - Then 'A' has 30 seconds to describe it to 'B'.
  - 'B' has one minute to instruct 'C' to build the object.
  - This can be done three times. 'A' cannot go back to the object after the third visit.
  - 'A' can now fetch the real object. Compare it with your group's construction.

# ARMCHAIR SCIENTISTS

**THINKING SKILL:** evaluation
**SUBJECT LINK:** science
**ORGANISATION:** whole class, sitting or standing outside
**RESOURCES:** none required

## WHAT TO DO

- Talk the following through slowly like a guided meditation.
- Explain that the children are going to use two of their senses to notice what's going on around them – and that this is a skill that scientists use.
- Ask them to close their eyes and listen. Pause.
- Ask, *What can you hear?* A car? Your heart? Your breathing? Someone moving? Bird song? Voices? Pause.
- Ask, *Which sound is the loudest?* Pause.
- Ask them to think about their bodies. What can they feel on the outside? The wind? Rain? Sunshine? Tight clothes? Pause.
- Which sensation do they think is strongest? Pause.
- What can they feel on the inside? Hunger? Thirst? A Pain? A feeling? Pause.
- Which feeling do they think is strongest? Pause.
- Now ask them to open their eyes and describe what they heard or felt to a partner.

## FLOWER PETALS

**THINKING SKILL:** evaluation
**SUBJECT LINK:** art
**LEARNING LINK:** visual
**ORGANISATION:** pairs
**RESOURCES:** 2cm and 5cm circles cut out from card – six circles per pair; sheets of card; blindfolds; pens; paper; glue sticks; scissors

### WHAT TO DO

● 'A' and 'B' have to sit back-to-back, next to a desk.
● 'A' sticks up to three circles on the paper (but doesn't let 'B' see how many). 'B' cuts out lots of petal shapes from the card, placing them on the desk for 'A' to stick around the circles to create flowers.
● When the petals are stuck down, 'B' puts on the blindfold and judges how many flowers there are and how many petals on each flower by feeling them.
● 'A' writes down how many 'B' says.
● 'B' takes off the blindfold and compares the picture with what has been written.
● 'A' and 'B' swap roles and try again. Each time a child judges the right amount of flowers and petals the other child throws their hands in the air and says *Rhododendron*.

### NOW TRY THIS

● Ask the children to cut out from card the outline of a familiar object (for example, a face in silhouette, a mug or a snake). Their partner identifies the object while blindfolded.
● Use different-textured material for the petals. For example, they could guess how many felt, tissue paper or card petals are on the flowers.

## WHAT HAPPENS IN WATER?

**THINKING SKILL:** reasoning
**SUBJECT LINK:** science
**LEARNING LINK:** visual, auditory
**ORGANISATION:** pairs and fours
**RESOURCES:** water in a large bowl or paddling pool; objects to place in the water, for example, a penny, a leaf, a cork, a small plastic boat; 'What happens if?' questions written on the board relating to investigating the effect of water:

*What happens if the penny is placed in the plastic boat?*
*What happens if I blow the leaf?*
*What happens if I press the leaf with my fingers?*
*What happens if I blow the cork?*
*What happens if I add more water?*
*What happens if the boat is turned upside down?*
*What happens if I put the penny on the leaf?*
*What happens if I put the cork on the leaf*

### WHAT TO DO

● Look at the *What happens if...* questions on the board.
● Take a minute to look at the water and the objects beside it.
● Place all or one of the objects in the water. Choose one of the questions.
● Write down or tell your partner what might happen.
● Act out doing the *What happens if...*
● When you are selected, come to the bowl and try it out – were you correct?
● With another pair, share your thinking.
● As a four, choose another *What happens if...* and answer it together.
● When you are chosen, come to the bowl and try it out.

# COLOUR RAINBOWS

**THINKING SKILL:** creative thinking
**SUBJECT LINK:** art
**LEARNING LINK:** visual
**ORGANISATION:** individuals
**RESOURCES:** template of a rainbow photocopied for each child; colouring pens/pencils/wax crayons in the following colours: red, orange, yellow, green, blue, indigo, violet (enough for each child); *Richard of York gave battle in vain* written on the board

## WHAT TO DO

● Do the children know what a rainbow is made from? (*raindrops*)
● Ask how many colours there are in a rainbow (*seven*).
● Do they know the colour order? Give the clue – the outer edge is red, the inside edge is violet.
● Explain that some people remember the order by saying *Richard of York gave battle in vain.*
● Ask the children to colour in their own rainbow. Can they think of their own phrase to help remember the colour order?

## NOW TRY THIS

Here are some ideas to make this into a more kinaesthetic exercise:
**1.** Do a Mexican wave with the children saying each colour of the rainbow in order.
**2.** Colour in a piece of A4 paper for each colour of the rainbow. Give this set to seven children. Tell them to jump into the shape of an arc saying their colour in order and holding it in the air.

# OLYMPICS 2012

**THINKING SKILL:** creative thinking
**SUBJECT LINK:** geography
**LEARNING LINK:** visual
**ORGANISATION:** individuals
**RESOURCES:** play dough or similar

## WHAT TO DO

● The Olympics are going to be held in London in 2012. Lots of people will visit Britain to see the Olympics and visit other places.
● Imagine that you have been asked to help support the Olympics by attracting visitors to your local area.
● Think for a minute about your local area and what it has to offer.

● Tell your neighbour one or two things – this could be special foods, buildings, sports facilities, activities, tourist spots – things that people would want to visit.
● You've now got two minutes to make your idea with play dough and get ready to explain it to the class.

# TWO NEW IDEAS

**THINKING SKILL:** creative thinking
**SUBJECT LINK:** design and technology
**LEARNING LINK:** visual
**ORGANISATION:** small groups
**RESOURCES:** a plain (cardboard or wooden) box or a plain fabric bag; A3 sheets; pencils; glue; a needle and thread; sticky tape; a variety of materials to add to the objects (beads, buttons, string, wool, fasteners, sequins); fabric pens or paint; other art and craft materials, such as fabric, card, different papers (optional)

## WHAT TO DO

● Give each group a box or bag. The groups need to look critically at it.
● They have to think of two ways to change or improve the object. They could:
  ● add something
  ● change or add a colour
  ● cut out a shape
● Go round each group and share ideas.
● Let them carry out their ideas and compare the finished products.

## NOW TRY THIS

**1.** If only one of the two changes could be made, which do the children think would be best?
**2.** If the resources are not available, use a picture of a plain set of drawers, for example, and ask the children to think of two ways to change or improve the item.
**3.** Alternatively, hand out copies of simple outlines of objects. Ask them to make two changes. The intention is to compare the finished drawings or ideas to see how many different ways there are to change an object.

# MAKE ME

**THINKING SKILL:** creative thinking
**SUBJECT LINK:** design and technology
**LEARNING LINK:** visual
**ORGANISATION:** whole class
**RESOURCES:** a small piece of Plasticine™ or similar for each child

## WHAT TO DO

• Tell the children that design and technology is about making things people want. It's important to say exactly what you want, so that the right thing gets made.
• Tell them you are going to describe something that you want. They have one minute to make it from their Plasticine™.
• After the minute is up, you will say, *Down*. They must put what they have made in the middle of the table.
• Explain that there may be lots of different ways to make what you ask for. Not everyone's work will look the same.
• Call out instructions such as:
  *make me something long and thin*
  *make me something very round*
  *make me a monster*
  *make me a face*
  *make me a hand*
  *make me something spiky*
  *make me a nose*
  *make me something with a hole in it*
  *make me something with at least one corner.*
• After each instruction, look at examples of what they have made.

# MATERIAL WORLD

**THINKING SKILL:** reasoning
**SUBJECT LINK:** design and technology
**LEARNING LINK:** kinaesthetic
**ORGANISATION:** groups
**RESOURCES:** a piece of coloured, patterned material for each group

## WHAT TO DO

• Lay out a piece of material in front of each group.
• Give them a couple of minutes to look at it. Discuss its colours and pattern.
• Now ask the groups to get hold of the material – everyone holding on lightly with two hands.

• Each person must now say *I like this material because…* and give a reason.
• As they say their sentence, they let go.
• When the last person has let go, everyone picks up the material again and repeats the activity.

## NOW TRY THIS

Substitute with *I don't like this material because…*, *This material is better than… .*

# OUT OF PLACE

**THINKING SKILL:** evaluation
**SUBJECT LINK:** history
**LEARNING LINK:** visual
**ORGANISATION:** pairs sitting in groups of four or six
**RESOURCES:** sets of pictures showing scenes, places and people associated with particular time periods, for example, the Roman, Tudor and Victorian periods. Replace one picture in each set with a picture from a different period

## WHAT TO DO

• Ask the children to look at the set of pictures.
• Explain they are all pictures from a historical period, but one does not fit in.
• Ask them what is the common theme that links all but one of the words in each set.
• They should find the odd one out and write it down on the paper, giving a reason.

## NOW TRY THIS

**1.** Ask the children to make the set complete by trading the odd one out with a picture that fits their set. They may need to trade a few times before getting the right picture.
**2.** Gather all the odd ones out. Can the children regroup them into their own sets?
**3.** Ask them to work with another one or two pairs and combine their pictures, putting them into new groups. They could be all in the same period or the groups could be based on other themes, such as clothes and buildings.
**4.** Use pictures for other subjects. For example, look at artistic styles and techniques to create new odd ones out.

# BAG A DESIGN AGAINST TIME

**THINKING SKILL:** reasoning
**SUBJECT LINK:** design and technology
**LEARNING LINK:** visual
**ORGANISATION:** small groups
**RESOURCES:** a selection of materials (for example, buttons, fabric, card, sugar paper, pipe cleaners, sequins, wool); string; sticky tape; a stapler; glue; starting points for bags (for example, plastic carrier bags, plain cloth bags, card, cardboard boxes)

## WHAT TO DO

● You have ten minutes to make a simple bag out of the materials.

● You need to consider the look and function of the bag, and its owner. What will it be used for? This will give guidance as to how strong the bag needs to be and how big.

● For example, if your bag is for keeping trunks and a small towel, it needs to be waterproof, to have space for those two items, and a handle to carry it. It doesn't need to be detailed or have intricate buttons or sequins, as these could get damaged in the changing rooms of a swimming pool.

● If you were designing an evening bag for the Queen to keep a spare pair of earrings in, your needs would be different!

● You will not have long to make the bag so work as a team. You will need to talk a lot and reason with each other. You should have a reason for every material you use.

● When the bag is finished, display it on the table.

● Then walk around the room and see other groups' bags.

# POWER QUESTIONS

**THINKING SKILL:** enquiry
**SUBJECT LINK:** science
**LEARNING LINK:** visual
**ORGANISATION:** pairs
**RESOURCES:** different objects to handle to stimulate children's thinking, for example, a lavender flower, a plastic bag, a light bulb, a piece of wire, an ice cube, a thermometer, a match, a mirror, a prism, a battery; pictures of different objects that the children can't handle in real life, for example, a tooth, a bee, a heart, a brain, bones, the sun, a parachute

## WHAT TO DO

● Some scientists only look for answers and some only look for questions. When you're a scientist, it's best to do both.

● Here are five power questions to help you think about science.

> *Power questions:*
> *What is it?*
> *What does it do?*
> *How can you use it?*
> *How is it made?*
> *What's better than it?*

● Working with a partner or on your own, choose one thing.

● Hold the object and examine it carefully. Then answer all five power questions with your partner.

## NOW TRY THIS

Choose an idea from one of your answers. See if you can ask the five questions again about that answer. For example, *What does a tooth do? It helps you break down food into smaller pieces.* Choose 'food' and ask the five questions again.

# FINGER COUNTING

**THINKING SKILL:** information processing
**SUBJECT LINK:** mathematics
**LEARNING LINK:** visual, auditory
**ORGANISATION:** pairs, whole class
**RESOURCES:** none required

## WHAT TO DO

● Explain that it is possible to count from one to ten using only the fingers on one hand, as illustrated below:

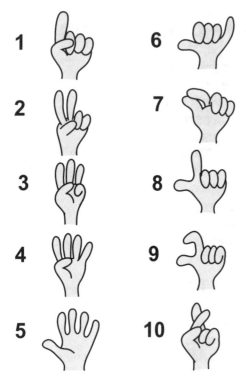

● Demonstrate this to the children and let them practise in pairs – counting up to ten and down again – saying each number as they make it – use copies of the illustration to help.

● Say numbers between one and ten at random to the whole class, asking the children to make the hand sign.

● Make a hand sign between one and ten to the whole class, asking the children to call out the number it represents.

● Once they've got the idea, do some of the following – as a whole class or in pairs:
  ● Count up and down the even numbers: 2, 4, 6, 8, 10, 8, 6, 4, 2
  ● Count up and down the odd numbers: 1, 3, 5, 7, 9, 7, 5, 3, 1

● Ask questions with answers between one and ten – children make hand-sign answers.

## NOW TRY THIS

**1.** Can they make numbers 11–20 using just one hand?

**2.** Can they make numbers over ten using the original signs but with both hands?
**3.** What numbers can two people working together make?

# MORE FINGER COUNTING

**THINKING SKILL:** information processing
**SUBJECT LINK:** mathematics
**LEARNING LINK:** visual, auditory
**ORGANISATION:** pairs, whole class
**RESOURCES:** none required

## WHAT TO DO

● Explain that it is possible to count from one to 16 using only the fingers on one hand. This is how to do it:

● Touch the thumb to the tip of the first finger (1); to the first segment of the first finger (2); the second segment (3); the third segment (4).

● Repeat with the tip and segments of the second finger (5, 6, 7, 8).

● Repeat with the third finger (9, 10, 11, 12) and little finger (13, 14, 15, 16).

● Demonstrate this to the children and let them practise in pairs – counting up to 16 and down again – saying each number as they make it.

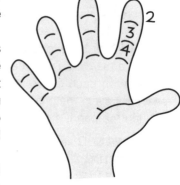

● Say numbers between one and 16 at random, asking the children to make the hand sign.

● Make a hand sign between one and 16, asking the children to call out the number it represents.

● Once they've got the idea, do some of the following – as a whole class or in pairs:
  ● Count up and down the even numbers: 2, 4, 6, 8, 10, 12, 14, 16, 14, 12, 10, 8, 6, 4, 2
  ● Count up and down the odd numbers: 1, 3, 5, 7, 9, 11, 13, 15, 13, 11, 9, 7, 5, 3, 1

● Ask questions with answers between one and 19 – the children make hand-sign answers.

## NOW TRY THIS

**1.** Ask the children how you could make the numbers 1–20 using the same method.
**2.** Ask them how you could make numbers over 16 using two hands.

# PICTURE PUZZLES

**THINKING SKILL:** enquiry
**SUBJECT LINK:** history
**LEARNING LINK:** visual
**ORGANISATION:** pairs
**RESOURCES:** a variety of colour pictures or photographs of any historical site, person, place or artefact for cutting up; card for backing; glue sticks; scissors

## WHAT TO DO

● Choose one person from each pair to collect a picture and piece of card.
● They have to stick the picture on to the card and then cut up the picture to make a puzzle for another pair. Ask them what sorts of shapes puzzle pieces are. How big will each piece be?
● Now they swap pieces with another pair. Can they put the pieces together?

## NOW TRY THIS

Each pair could write clues for their puzzle.

# FINGER STORY

**THINKING SKILL:** reasoning, creative thinking
**SUBJECT LINK:** literacy
**LEARNING LINK:** visual, auditory
**ORGANISATION:** pairs
**RESOURCES:** a piece of paper for each child with the following words scattered over it (each one ringed): I, forest, witch, path, water, spell, evil, good, brave, snow, leaves, house, boy, snake, you, beautiful, quickly, slowly, awful, rude, he, she, then, soon, next, suddenly, later, once, monster, cave, disappear

## WHAT TO DO

● Give the children a few minutes to familiarise themselves with the words.
● Ask them to choose a finger and touch each word as you say it.
● Read out the words, slowly, one at a time.
● Tell them that the words come from a story yet to be told – a story they are going to tell!

● Ask them to begin a story, touching each word as they say it.
● They don't need to use all of the words and each word can be touched as often as is needed.
● You may want to give an example: *Once, there was a beautiful witch who lived in the forest...*
● Remind them to take turns – maybe swapping after every sentence, or when one person's ideas dry up.

## NOW TRY THIS

**1.** Create new word sheets by borrowing selections of words from existing stories.
**2.** Limit the use of each word – three times maximum, twice or even only once.
**3.** Number the words and ask them to create a story using the words in strict order.

# I CAN FEEL IT

**THINKING SKILL:** information processing
**SUBJECT LINK:** science
**LEARNING LINK:** auditory
**ORGANISATION:** pairs
**RESOURCES:** objects linked to science – magnifying glass, flower, Newtonmeter, thermometer and so on (take appropriate safety precautions); one blindfold per pair

## WHAT TO DO

● Decide who is 'A' and 'B'.
● 'B' fixes on their blindfold while 'A' comes to collect an object.
● 'A' gives the object to 'B' who attempts to identify it by touch.
● 'B' can ask up to three questions but cannot ask directly what it is.
● Allow up to two minutes before 'A' and 'B' swap, 'B' collecting another object.

## NOW TRY THIS

**1.** Allow the children to use only one hand.
**2.** Ask them to put on gloves and repeat with a different object.

# RIGHT HAND–LEFT HAND

**THINKING SKILL:** enquiry, creative thinking
**SUBJECT LINK:** art
**LEARNING LINK:** visual
**ORGANISATION:** whole class, pairs
**RESOURCES:** charcoal and A3 paper for each child; kitchen utensils displayed on a table, for example, a knife, a fork, a spoon, a corkscrew, a can opener, scissors, a cheese grater; blindfolds

## WHAT TO DO

● Point to the kitchen items and ask the children to name them. In pairs, ask them to choose one object and put it in front of them.
● Tell them they are going to draw the object with the hand they do not normally write with. They can pick up the object, and examine it in detail before they start.
● Does it feel heavy or light? How big is it? Does it have sharp points? Does it cast a shadow on the table? Ask them to notice the dark and light shades of colour.
● Ask them to draw the object with their left hand if they are right-handed and their right hand if they are left-handed.
● They should then compare their sketches with those of their neighbours.

## NOW TRY THIS

**1.** They should draw the same object on the same piece of paper wearing a blindfold.
**2.** They should draw the object from a different perspective, a bird's-eye view for instance.

# SCISSORS, PAPER, PAINTBRUSH

**THINKING SKILL:** reasoning, creative thinking, enquiry
**SUBJECT LINK:** art
**LEARNING LINK:** auditory
**ORGANISATION:** pairs
**RESOURCES:** scissors; paper; a paintbrush

## WHAT TO DO

● In the well-known hand game, 'stone – paper – scissors', two players (on the count of three) simultaneously make either a pair of scissors (two fingers), a piece of paper (flat hand) or a stone (fist). The result is either a draw (both players making the same object) or one player wins (scissors cut paper; paper wraps stone

and so on).
● Teach the game to the children but replace the stone with a paintbrush – the hand symbol being a pointed first finger.
● The children must reason about the rules – does paper beat paintbrush? Do scissors lose to paper?
● Play the game for a few minutes, then suggest rules or alterations based on experience.

## NOW TRY THIS

Choose three or more objects and actions related to other subject areas, for example, science: water, oil, stone, cork.

# TOUCHY FEELY SHAPES

**THINKING SKILL:** evaluation
**SUBJECT LINK:** art, design and technology
**ORGANISATION:** pairs
**RESOURCES:** a variety of 3D shapes including different types of packages, for example, a cube, cuboid, prism, cone, pyramid, cylinder, triangular prism; drawstring 'feely' bags containing a variety of 3D shapes (enough for each pair)

## WHAT TO DO

● Look at all the 3D shapes. Can you name any? Pick them up and examine them. Is any of the packaging familiar? What would the contents be used for? Could you eat them?
● Your partner collects a feely bag. One of you put your hand inside and feel each shape to identify them without looking.
● The other one asks how many edges has each shape got? How many sides?
● Discuss what each one is and bring them out of the bag one at a time.
● What did you find?
● Swap bags with another pair. Swap roles: asking the questions or feeling the shapes.

## NOW TRY THIS

Collect as many 3D shapes as you can from home. Bring them into school. Label each one for a display.

# MATCH CITY

**THINKING SKILL:** reasoning, creative thinking
**SUBJECT LINK:** geography
**LEARNING LINK:** auditory, visual
**ORGANISATION:** pairs
**RESOURCES:** ten matchsticks and five counters for each pair

## WHAT TO DO

● Counters are cities and matches are roads. You are going to connect your cities together.
● Take it in turns to place a city or a road (counter or match).
● There are two rules: each move must make a connection (except for the first go for each player) and any two cities can only be joined by one road.
● When all the counters and matches have been played, work out a route to visit every city with the least number of moves. One move is one road (match).

## NOW TRY THIS

Alter the numbers of matches and counters used to set up the network.

# HAND OVER THE MONEY

**THINKING SKILL:** information processing
**SUBJECT LINK:** mathematics
**ORGANISATION:** pairs of similar mathematics ability
**RESOURCES:** plastic or real money; blindfolds

## WHAT TO DO

● Give the children a few minutes to handle the money and become familiar with how it feels.
● Ask them to close their eyes and try to recognise each coin by touch.
● Ask the pairs to choose who is 'A' and who is 'B'.
● 'B' puts on the blindfold.
● 'A' hands a coin to 'B' and asks them to identify it.
● 'A' collects several coins, less than 10p and using two or three coins.
● 'A' hands the money to 'B' who has to work out how much they have been given by identifying the coins and adding up the amounts.
● Swap the blindfold and repeat.

## NOW TRY THIS

As the children become better at identifying the coins, increase the number and the amounts.

# CONSEQUENCES

**THINKING SKILL:** information processing, creative thinking
**SUBJECT LINK:** literacy
**LEARNING LINK:** visual
**ORGANISATION:** groups of six
**RESOURCES:** a piece of A4 paper for each child

## WHAT TO DO

● The well-known game of consequences allows each person to secretly contribute part of a drawing – only at the end of the game is the final creation revealed.
● Use this idea to generate ideas in literacy.
● Each child writes down any fairy tale character at the top of their paper, then folds it over so that it's hidden.
● Pass the folded paper round to the next child who adds a place.
● Keep going, adding the following three things: a villain, a problem, a hero.
● When each paper is opened, it will show ideas that could stimulate a story – for example:

> *Character – Goldilocks*
> *Place – by the river*
> *Villain – a wicked witch*
> *Problem – the weather is stolen*
> *Hero – Prince Charming*

## NOW TRY THIS

Apply the consequences idea to other subjects. For example: design and technology: create requirements for a new object – a chair: number of legs/size/type of fabric/where it's used/what it's made of.

# COLLAGE CREATION

**THINKING SKILL:** creative thinking
**SUBJECT LINK:** art
**LEARNING LINK:** auditory, visual
**ORGANISATION:** pairs
**RESOURCES:** relaxing classical music, such as *Moonlight Sonata Opus 27, No 2* (1801) by Ludwig Van Beethoven or *Symphony No 1 in D Major – Titan* by Gustav Mahler; a variety of magazines/colour supplements; A3 paper; glue sticks

## WHAT TO DO

● One person from each pair chooses two or three magazines.
● Close your eyes, sit back in your chair, relax your arms, your legs and think about your breathing while listening to the music.
● Is the music loud, soft, gentle, sharp, scary or boisterous?
● What sort of colours does it make you think of, perhaps loud, angry music, makes you see red, and sad, gentle music makes you feel blue.
● Open your eyes and start to tear images and colours from the magazines. Stick them on your paper to make a collage. You can make a picture or just use colours to match the mood of the music.

## NOW TRY THIS

**1.** Use different types of music to see how music can affect mood. Are your collage creations different for classical and rock music?
**2.** After a collage session, talk about why you chose particular colours. Write a caption to describe your colour choice.

# SLAP MATHS

**THINKING SKILL:** information processing
**SUBJECT LINK:** mathematics
**LEARNING LINK:** visual
**ORGANISATION:** pairs of similar mathematics ability
**RESOURCES:** digit cards zero to nine for each pair

## WHAT TO DO

● Tell the children they will need quick reflexes and to work carefully in pairs.

● They should lay the cards in order on the table.
● Read out some questions whose answers are between zero and nine. When they know the answer, they should place their hand on (or slap) the card.
● If their partner gets there just before, they have won.
● They should choose one hand to slap with and start with hands on knees.
● Start off with the following questions:
  ● 18 divided by 6
  ● 8 subtracted from 16
  ● 5 add 3
  ● 30 divided by 10
  ● 45 divided by 5.

## NOW TRY THIS

**1.** Ask the children to use their other hand.
**2.** Have two-digit answers requiring the slapping of two cards, for example, *two times nine,* slap one and eight.
**3.** Adapt the activity for other subjects with numerical answers, for example, *How many legs does an octopus have?*
**4.** Peg cards on a washing line and get the children to stand up to grab them.

# SWINGING STRING

**THINKING SKILL:** creative thinking, reasoning
**SUBJECT LINK:** art
**LEARNING LINK:** auditory
**ORGANISATION:** pairs
**RESOURCES:** A3 paper; two pencils tied together by a 15cm length of string

## WHAT TO DO

● Children will need a reasonable level of cooperative skill to do this activity.
● They will draw together with their pencils connected by string.
● Children decide who is 'A' and who is 'B' and sit next to each other.

- First, 'B' holds the pencil still on the paper.
- 'A' starts to draw an animal, but must not make their partner's pencil move by pulling too hard ('A' will have to draw within a circle determined by the string's length).
- After one minute, call out *Freeze*, 'A' must leave the pencil exactly where it is. 'B' takes over – drawing an object that could be near the animal (for example, a stable for a horse) – not pulling their partner's pencil out of place.
- After another minute, ask 'A' to take over and draw the sky.
- Continue, adding to the picture – fields, people, and so on.

## NOW TRY THIS

1. Set rules such as: the final picture must go to each edge of the paper.
2. Link to different subjects – draw story characters; science experiments; an orchestra.

# THINKY LINKS

**THINKING SKILL:** reasoning
**SUBJECT LINK:** geography, history
**LEARNING LINK:** visual, auditory
**ORGANISATION:** groups of three
**RESOURCES:** nine Multilink™ cubes (or similar) for each group – each child needs one set of three Multilink™ cubes, all the same colour

## WHAT TO DO

- Explain that ideas can link together – all you need is a place to start and a way to join them.
- Explain that they are going to think about transport. If you start with bus, there are lots of ideas that can link to it – wheels, fare, passenger, driver, bus stop and so on.
- Explain that when they have chosen their second idea, they can link another one – so if they chose fare, they could choose money.
- Taking it in turn, ask them to start at bus and link ideas. They each add a piece of Multilink™ to show that they linked an idea.

- They keep going until everyone has linked three ideas – the Multilink™ can become any shape they want.
- Now ask them to break up the Multilink™ and start with another idea: farmer or soldier or bread – and repeat.

# THINKING HINGES

**THINKING SKILL:** enquiry, information processing
**SUBJECT LINK:** PSHE
**ORGANISATION:** pairs
**RESOURCES:** a small piece of card for each child, for example, a quarter of A4

## WHAT TO DO

- Give each child a piece of card. Show them how to fold it in half. The fold makes a hinge which can be moved.
- Ask each child to draw a simple face (showing some emotion) on one half of the inside of the card, and then close it.
- Keeping the cards closed, the pairs swap.
- On the count of three, children open their partner's card and on the other half of the inside, draw the opposite emotion.
- Ask the children to share answers. How accurate were the drawings?
- Repeat using the outside of the card.

## NOW TRY THIS

Apply to other subject areas, for example, mathematics questions and answers, book titles and authors, countries and capital cities.

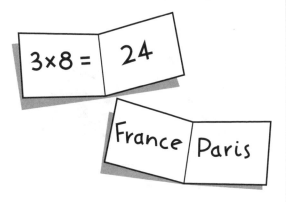

# KINAESTHETIC LEARNING

## TRACING WORDS

**THINKING SKILL:** evaluation, information processing
**SUBJECT LINK:** literacy
**ORGANISATION:** pairs
**RESOURCES:** pen and paper

### WHAT TO DO
- Ask the children to say words containing the letter string *igh*, like light and sight. Write their suggestions on the board.
- Label each pair 'A' and 'B'.
- 'A' has to think of an *igh* word, write it down without 'B' seeing it, and place it face down.
- 'A' then traces the first letter of the word on their partner's back and then the following letters in turn. When 'B' recognises the word they say it aloud.
- If 'B' is incorrect, 'A' says *Try again* and traces the word again. 'B' can keep trying to guess the word.
- If 'B' is correct, 'A' says *Yes* and shows 'B' the word.
- 'A' and 'B' can swap over each time one of them guesses the word correctly.

### NOW TRY THIS
Do the same for another letter string, such as *ough* or *ai*.

## OPPOSITES

**THINKING SKILL:** creative thinking
**SUBJECT LINK:** literacy
**ORGANISATION:** pairs
**RESOURCES:** pen and paper; two lists of ten words for each pair that they can act out, for example:

| | |
|---|---|
| high | happy |
| sad | huge |
| heavy | light |
| blunt | calm |
| grumpy | alive |
| smile | sensible |
| cold | short |
| tall | push |
| tiny | sweet |
| push | hot |

### WHAT TO DO
- Tell the children that they are going to play a game about opposite words and their meanings.
- Ask them to act *hot*. Do they know what the opposite of hot is? Ask them to act it.
- Split the pairs into 'A' and 'B'.
- Give all the 'B's a list of ten words, and a pen and paper to the 'A's.
- 'B' has to read the first word on the list (not out loud) and act out the opposite.
- 'A' must watch carefully and write down what action or word 'B' is acting out, numbering the list one to ten.
- 'B' carries on acting out the opposite of each word without talking. 'A' must record what the word or action is.

- Compare the two lists. Are the words all opposites?

### NOW TRY THIS
Repeat the activity with a new list. 'A' now does the acting and 'B' the guessing.

# BALANCE

**THINKING SKILL:** creative thinking
**SUBJECT LINK:** PE
**LEARNING LINK:** auditory
**ORGANISATION:** whole class
**RESOURCES:** recording of any Baroque music (such as Rameau), harpsichord music (by Bach, for example) or a flute concerto by Mozart

## WHAT TO DO

● Start playing the relaxing music (to help the children focus).
● Tell them to find a place to stand facing a wall and listen.
● They need to focus on a point on the wall and stand on one leg for as long as possible.
● When they've found their balance, ask them to raise their right arm in the air.
● Next, they scratch their nose with their left hand.
● Now say, *Stick out your tongue!*
● Remind everyone to keep balanced on one leg. If they find this difficult, they can stand on the other leg.
● Tell everyone to say, *I'm standing on one leg, with my right arm in the air, scratching my nose.*

# SING-A-LONG-A-NOTE

**THINKING SKILL:** reasoning, information processing
**SUBJECT LINK:** music
**LEARNING LINK:** visual, auditory
**ORGANISATION:** groups of three or four
**RESOURCES:** separate drawings of musical notes each on A4 paper – several of each per group, for example, minim = 2 beats, crotchet = 1 beat, quaver = ½ beat, semi quaver = ¼ beat; Blu-Tack™

## WHAT TO DO

● Split the children into groups of three or four.
● Hand out a variety of the musical notes to each group.

● Write a number on the board. Ask them to find the notes adding up to that number and then clap, stamp, or drum the number of beats.
● When they have the answer, they wave their hands in the air.
● A volunteer from the first group to find the answer sticks the correct notes on the board or writes the sequence. For example, 1 + 2 = 3, or ♩ + ♩ = 3.

# GREETINGS

**THINKING SKILL:** information processing, creative thinking
**SUBJECT LINK:** modern languages, PSHE
**LEARNING LINK:** auditory
**ORGANISATION:** pairs
**RESOURCES:** none required

## WHAT TO DO

● Ask the children how people greet each other all over the world.
● They find out or invent as many ways of greeting someone as they can.
● Encourage them to stand up and act out greetings.
● Challenge them by asking them to use no words in their greetings and then to include foreign languages.
● Here are some examples:
  ● Bonjour, Salut (kissing on each cheek – French)
  ● Give me five (slap hands together – USA, Caribbean)
  ● Hello, Hi, Good morning (shake hands – UK)
  ● (rubbing noses – Inuit/Eskimos)

## NOW TRY THIS

Ask the children to create a greeting with set criteria. For example, the greeting must involve: only one arm and hand; a single sound; a facial expression that makes the other person feel welcome.

# CIRCUS TRICKS 1

**THINKING SKILL:** reasoning
**SUBJECT LINK:** literacy, PE
**LEARNING LINK:** visual
**ORGANISATION:** pairs
**RESOURCES:** numbered labels of circus performers, for example: I am a juggler, I am a fire eater, I am a trapeze artist, I am a clown, I am a tightrope walker, I am a lion tamer; pen and paper

## WHAT TO DO

● Tell the children that a circus is auditioning for new members. Are there any volunteers?
● Before they can audition, you need to check that they understand each role, what they need to do and what they need to have.
● Pass round the labels to volunteers for the auditions. They cannot reveal their role to anyone.
● The children take turns, starting with number one, to perform their roles. The rest of the class guesses the act.
● The class then guess what prop the performer is using and anything else that is needed, such as a safety net for a trapeze artist.
● The performer mimes as many things that they think are needed for the act. Limit the time allowed for each mime.
● Encourage them to use language such as, *I think it's a lion tamer because he's cracking a whip* – giving reasons for guesses.

# CIRCUS TRICKS 2

**THINKING SKILL:** creative thinking
**SUBJECT LINK:** PE
**LEARNNG LINK:** visual
**ORGANISATION:** pairs
**RESOURCES:** space in a room; pictures of circus performers, such as tightrope walker, juggler, lion tamer, acrobat, and so on

## WHAT TO DO

● Imagine being part of a circus. What act would you perform?

● One of you is 'A' and the other is 'B'. Who do we see at the circus? What do they do?
● 'A' goes first, miming a circus act or trick. 'B' writes down what 'A' is doing.
● There is no speaking because it is a mime act. You should use the whole of your body.
● Swap over when 'B' has guessed what 'A' is doing.

## NOW TRY THIS

**1.** Talk about different circuses such as the *Moscow State Circus* that does not include animals and is famous for acrobatics. Can you think of other circus acts that don't involve animals?
**2.** Create a new circus act that combines two or more existing ones.

# EXCUSEZ-MOI?

**THINKING SKILL:** evaluation, information processing
**SUBJECT LINK:** modern languages
**LEARNING LINK:** auditory
**ORGANISATION:** pairs
**RESOURCES:** a list of animal names in French and English written on the board; a cow – une vache, a duck – un canard, a horse – un cheval, a cat – un chat, a dog – un chien

## WHAT TO DO

● Today you are going to think about sound.
● Think about the sounds you can make, like whistling, singing, clapping.
● Decide who is 'A' and who is 'B'.
● 'A' makes an animal sound and mimes the animal's movements. 'B' has to guess the animal.
● When 'B' has guessed, they say the animal in French, then you can move on to the next sound.
● If you are not sure what the animal is, you can ask, *Excusez-moi?*
● How many animal sounds and movements can you recognise? Did you know the names in French?
● Think about the French and English words for each animal – which do you prefer?

# MOVE ABOUT ODD ONE OUT

**THINKING SKILL:** evaluation, reasoning
**SUBJECT LINK:** PE
**LEARNING LINK:** auditory
**ORGANISATION:** whole class
**RESOURCES:** the following sets of words:
1. balance, hover, poise, control, topple; 2. breathe, lungs, gasp, inhale, respire; 3. run, sprint, jog, skip, dart; 4. fall, jump, spring, leap, vault; 5. dance, sing, bop, boogie, jig

## WHAT TO DO

● Listen to these sets of words one at a time. The groups of words have similar meanings, yet one of the words in each set does not match the others.
● Do the actions, if possible, and find the odd one out.

## NOW TRY THIS

If you have time, you could think up some of your own words including an odd one out. Give them to another pair to work out.

> **ANSWERS**
> 1. topple   2. lungs   3. skip   4. fall   5. sing
> Children will come up with equally plausible alternatives. Value all answers and all reasoning, leading the children to understand that each word can be the odd one out, if you pick the right criteria.

# FREEZE-FRAME

**THINKING SKILL:** creative thinking
**SUBJECT LINK:** PE
**LEARNING LINK:** visual
**ORGANISATION:** whole class
**RESOURCES:** space to sit in a large circle

## WHAT TO DO

● Get everyone to sit in a circle on the floor.
● Ask for a volunteer to be 'the actor'.
● Ask them to stand in the middle and mime a job, hobby or sport; it can be anything, for example, a ballerina or racing driver.
● Say *Freeze!* and point to someone else who asks the actor, *What are you doing?*
● The actor has to say something that is different from their action, for example, *I'm a swimmer*.
● The person who asked the question comes into the circle and takes on the same position as the first actor.
● When you say *Action!*, the new actor has to mime the occupation or action the previous actor said.
● Continue as before until everyone in the circle has had a go.

# TARGET TREE

**THINKING SKILL:** information processing
**SUBJECT LINK:** art
**LEARNING LINK:** visual, tactile
**ORGANISATION:** individuals, pairs
**RESOURCES:** for each child: two sheets of paper or card; felt-tipped pens or coloured crayons; scissors; glue sticks

## WHAT TO DO

● Think about what you would like to do before you are old.
● Where do you see yourself? Are you surfing on a beach in Tahiti?
● Have you been to university?
● Are you working? What kind of job are you doing?
● On one sheet of paper, draw five leaves and cut them out.
● On the other sheet, draw a tree with branches. On each leaf write or draw something you would like to do in the future.
● Stick your leaves on your tree and colour it all in.
● Show a partner your ideas.
● Mime all the things you want to do before you grow old, like swimming with dolphins. Can your partner guess them? Remember, no talking!

# MIMING MUSIC

**THINKING SKILL:** information processing
**SUBJECT LINK:** music
**LEARNING LINK:** kinaesthetic
**ORGANISATION:** individual
**RESOURCES:** recording of 'The Only Way is Up' by Yazz (Big Life), or other music with a strong beat; space for the children to stand and move around; a list of music-related questions, for example:

If a violinist plays the violin, what does a flautist play?
If a cellist plays the cello, what does a pianist play?
If an oboist plays the oboe, what does a trombonist play?
If a trombonist plays the trombone, what does a percussionist play?
Give an example of a brass instrument.
How would you play a steel drum?

## WHAT TO DO

● Explain that you are going to play musical statues with a difference.
● Tell the children that each time the music stops, they need to stand still and that you will ask a musical question.
● They need to answer by miming the instrument.

# WHO AND WHAT?

**THINKING SKILL:** reasoning
**SUBJECT LINK:** history
**LEARNING LINK:** visual
**ORGANISATION:** groups of three or four
**RESOURCES:** sets of pictures/photographs of people, places and objects connected to children's previous learning (one different set for each group), for example: a set of Roman pictures, Egyptian pictures, Saxon pictures

## WHAT TO DO

● Mix up the sets of pictures so that the new sets include pictures from different periods of history.
● Allocate a set of pictures and a different period of history (related to the pictures) to each group. For example, the first group might be the Roman team.
● Each group collects all the photos relating to their period in history.
● They need to move around the room and barter with other groups to get the photographs they need to make a complete set. They should exchange on a one-to-one basis.
● Continue until everyone has a complete set.

# WHOSE BODY IS IT ANYWAY?

**THINKING SKILL:** creative thinking
**SUBJECT LINK:** art
**LEARNING LINK:** visual
**ORGANISATION:** pairs
**RESOURCES:** a selection of colour supplements and magazines; art materials from the resource bank such as wool, straws, wire, felt, sequins, buttons; scissors; glue sticks; A4 paper

## WHAT TO DO

● Tell the children they are going to create a new person from the materials on the table. They should choose a selection of materials.
● Their new person can be as wacky as they like. They can cut out body parts from the magazines and add other materials to it, then stick each bit on the paper and see what person emerges. For example, they might cut out a ballerina's legs, a boxer's body and Wellington boots from a magazine and add wool for hair.
● Share all the pictures, cut them out, frame them with a cardboard border and display in a gallery on the wall, or on their desks!
● Set a time limit and encourage collaboration between children – maybe suggesting that one person does the upper body, the other person the lower.

## NOW TRY THIS

Ask them to do the same with animals. What is the strangest looking animal they can create?

# HEY YOU!

**THINKING SKILL:** information processing
**SUBJECT LINK:** PE
**LEARNING LINK:** auditory
**ORGANISATION:** whole class
**RESOURCES:** a copy of the poem 'Action rhymes for gaining attention' from *The ALPS Approach Resource Book: accelerated learning in primary schools* by Alistair Smith and Nicola Call (Network Educational Press Ltd)

*Point to the ceiling, point to the floor,*
*Point to the window, point to the door,*
*Point to you, point to me,*
*And turn and listen, quietly.*

*Touch your lips, touch your knees,*
*Touch your ears, now listen, please!*

*Give me one, give me two,*
*Give me five, look at you,*
*Ready to listen, ready to see,*
*Ready to learn, now look at me.*

*Hands on your head, fingers on your nose,*
*Thumbs on your ears, wiggle your toes,*
*Point to your friend, point to your chair,*
*Point to the teacher, hands in the air.*
*Hands on your head, fingers on your nose,*
*Thumbs on your ears, lips firmly closed.*

## WHAT TO DO

● Ask the children how many ways there are of getting attention from a teacher, for example, waving hands or calling out. What different ways does the teacher gain attention from children?
● Read the poem aloud. Explain that it is an action rhyme. They need to listen carefully, watch the actions and join in when they can.
● Ask everyone to stand up and go through the actions together. Repeat the rhyme as many times as you wish.

## NOW TRY THIS

**1.** Make up some more actions or extend existing ones to suit your class. You could play music to accompany the actions.
**2.** Explore how rhyme is used in the poem, is it effective and why? (It is written in rhyming couplets.)
**3.** Try singing 'Heads, Shoulders, Knees and Toes' with the actions.
**4.** Agree a set of class movements to use for being silent; lining up; sitting on the carpet, and so on.

# IF THE HAT FITS

**THINKING SKILL:** creative thinking
**SUBJECT LINK:** drama
**ORGANISATION:** groups of three or four
**RESOURCES:** a selection of hats

## WHAT TO DO

● One person from the group chooses a hat from the selection, with their eyes closed. They open their eyes, put the hat on and act in a 'style' that fits the hat. For example, a child choosing a big fancy hat could act like a posh lady.
● Keep the acts short so that each child can have a go.

## NOW TRY THIS

Use the hats in small group role-plays. Everyone in a group starts with a hat, but after about 30 seconds, they swap. They then continue their actions in a different style.

# BODY PATTERNS

**THINKING SKILL:** reasoning
**SUBJECT LINK:** mathematics
**LEARNING LINK:** visual
**ORGANISATION:** whole class, split into three equal-sized groups – 'A', 'B' and 'C'
**RESOURCES:** space for whole class to move in and line up

## WHAT TO DO

● Explain that they are going to make some patterns using their hands and bodies.
● All the 'A's fold their arms and keep them folded.
● All the 'B's put their hands on their shoulders and keep them there.
● All the 'C's put their hands by their sides and make fists.
● Without talking, they should line up in a pattern that goes: fists, folded, shoulders, fists, folded, shoulders…
● No talking is allowed.

# SHAKE IT ALL ABOUT

**THINKING SKILL:** information processing
**SUBJECT LINK:** PE, drama
**LEARNING LINK:** auditory
**ORGANISATION:** whole class
**RESOURCES:** space to move

## WHAT TO DO

● Ask the children to find a space to stand in. Explain that this activity warms up all the muscles in the body.

● Ask them to watch what you do and join in as soon as they can. Count to ten quickly, shaking your right hand at the same time, then count to ten again but shake your left hand instead. Repeat for the right leg and then the left leg.

● Repeat this activity with each hand and leg but counting one less for each round, until you are only counting one while shaking your right hand, one shaking your left hand and so on.

## NOW TRY THIS

The fewer numbers you count the quicker the activity. The children could add other moves, shaking heads or twitching noses. This can become hilarious as the counting gets faster!

# HUMAN XYLOPHONE

**THINKING SKILL:** enquiry
**SUBJECT LINK:** music
**LEARNING LINK:** auditory
**ORGANISATION:** groups of eight
**RESOURCES:** a large keyboard from middle C to high C (one octave) drawn on a roll of paper and stuck on the floor (each key should be labelled with the relevant letter); a piano, keyboard or xylophone

## WHAT TO DO

● Starting at middle C, play the scale of C major – one octave on a piano or keyboard.

● Tell the children each of them will be a note on that scale.

● All the middle Cs get together, all the Ds group together and so on.

● Play each note in turn and ask the relevant group to sing their note and keep it in their heads.

● The children can hum the notes quietly if they find it easier to remember the notes that way.

● One person from each group stands behind their notes. Starting at middle C and moving along to high C, each child jumps on to their note and sings or hums their note like a rising scale.

● Take it in turns so a child from each group has a go at humming and jumping on to their note at the same time.

● If someone is out of tune or sings the wrong note, what happens?

## NOW TRY THIS

**1.** Ask the children to jump on to the notes faster and faster so the scale goes up quickly and then try going back down the scale singing or humming the note and jumping off the note to the original starting position.

**2.** 'Play' and hum a simple tune like 'Merrily we roll along' by calling out the notes and the children copying.

# MAKING A NUMBER

**THINKING SKILL:** evaluation
**SUBJECT LINK:** mathematics
**LEARNING LINK:** visual, auditory
**ORGANISATION:** groups of five or six, standing in lines
**RESOURCES:** digit cards zero to nine for each group

## WHAT TO DO

● Share the cards out so each child has one or two cards. They hold one card in each hand.

● Each child keeps the same cards for this game.

● Explain that they are going to make different numbers and answer questions by showing their cards.

● They may have to swap places with other members of the group or poke their card in between other cards.

● Allow a few seconds for them to talk about what they have to do and rearrange themselves each time.

● Instruct groups as follows (adapt to ability):
  ● Hold your cards up in order, zero to nine.
  ● Hold your cards up in reverse order, nine to zero.
  ● Make the number 37,840.
  ● Make the number 12,965.
  ● Select five digits. Create the highest value number you can with them.
  ● Use the remaining five digits. Make the lowest value number with them.
  ● Hold up the prime numbers.
  ● Create a square number.
  ● Show me a number that is greater than 6000 and less than 6252.

# PASS IT ON

**THINKING SKILL:** information processing
**SUBJECT LINK:** music
**LEARNING LINK:** auditory, visual
**ORGANISATION:** groups of three or four
**RESOURCES:** none required

## WHAT TO DO

● Groups sit in a circle so they can all see each other. Explain that this is an action activity. They are going to take it in turns to say one musical thing they can do or a fact connected with music.
● Tell them that they should always look the person in the eye when they speak to them and when they have said their fact, pass on to their neighbour by gesturing with a part of the body. So, they might nod their head, wiggle their finger, point with their foot, or raise their eyebrows, or even just wink!

## NOW TRY THIS

Ask the children to come up with their own ideas. Remind them to use as many parts of their body as they can. No touching!

# MULTIPLICATION MOVES

**THINKING SKILL:** creative thinking
**SUBJECT LINK:** mathematics
**LEARNING LINK:** auditory
**ORGANISATION:** groups
**RESOURCES:** a relevant multiplication chart

## WHAT TO DO

● You are going to work in a group with people who are learning the same multiplication chart as you.
● Make sure that you can see the relevant chart.
● You are going to create a movement for each answer in the table.
● If you are learning the four-times table you will need to create a move for numbers 4, 8, 12, 16, 20, 24, 28, 32, 36, 40, 44 and 48.
● The movement has to be different for each number.
● Here are some ideas for you: hop, jump, march, wave, balance, walk, arm movement, head movement.
● When you have created the moves, your teacher will choose a group and rehearse the chart while saying the relevant times table.

# SHIPWRECKED

**THINKING SKILL:** creative thinking, reasoning, enquiry
**SUBJECT LINK:** PE, drama
**LEARNING LINK:** auditory
**ORGANISATION:** groups of three or four
**RESOURCES:** a large space; pictures of bread, biscuits and sandwiches; a five-litre bottle of water; a handful of plasters from a floating first aid kit; a pair of scissors; three matches in a matchbox, a piece of string and a personal CD player (one set of resources per group)

## WHAT TO DO

● Tell the children they have been shipwrecked on an island. They have just the items on the table with them.
● Each group has five minutes to create a tableau showing each item in use.
● As each group poses, the rest of the class select a person and guess what they are doing – for example, *Simon, are you using the CD to reflect the sun and signal across the beach?*
● Children in the tableau can only answer *Yes* or *No*.

# YUMMY ME

**THINKING SKILL:** reasoning, information processing
**SUBJECT LINK:** modern languages
**LEARNING LINK:** visual
**ORGANISATION:** table groups
**RESOURCES:** paper plates; flags and country labels – one for each group; a variety of pictures and labels of food from around the world – one set for each group (ensure that these can be matched to the flags and country labels); a simple world map for each table, enlarged to A3

## WHAT TO DO

● One person from your table should choose a country label and a flag to stick on the table.
● Look at your set of pictures and labels of foods from around the world. Find the right table for each food and place it on the table. You will need to look at the other groups' tables.
● On your map of the world label the continents and draw items of food for countries that you know.

## NOW TRY THIS

Draw a selection of these foods on paper plates. Design the flag for that country on a sticky label and stick it on your plate.

KINAESTHETIC LEARNING

# TECHY HOT SEAT

**THINKING SKILL:** reasoning
**SUBJECT LINK:** ICT
**LEARNING LINK:** auditory
**ORGANISATION:** whole class in a semicircle, apart from one chair, which faces the others or one 'hot-seat' at the front
**RESOURCES:** a timer

## WHAT TO DO

● Get the children to count around the semicircle, beginning with one for the first child, two for the second, and so on – the order in which they will go to the hot seat.

● Tell them to think about new technology, like mobile phones, computers, digital cameras. You want to hear their opinions on these things. They can only give an opinion when they are in the hot seat.

● Decide which aspect of new technology you want them to think about.

● Give them a minute in silence to think what they will say.

● Challenge them to see how fast everyone in the circle can give their opinions in the hot seat. The rules are:

● They have to walk quickly and safely to the hot seat – in order – starting with number one.

● If anyone runs or pushes they have to wait five seconds before the next person can sit in the hot seat.

● They can move to sit in the hot seat once the previous person is back in their seat.

● When on the seat, they make one statement, saying whether the new technology is good or bad and why. For example, *Mobile phones are good because you can call for help wherever you are.*

# BODY PARTS

**THINKING SKILL:** evaluation
**SUBJECT LINK:** PE, dance
**ORGANISATION:** pairs
**RESOURCES:** a large space; a CD by the group Oasis

## WHAT TO DO

● Ask the pairs to choose a starting position where one part of their body is touching another part of their partner's body – they could be standing, lying on the floor, curled up or crouching back to back.

● When the music starts they should move around in the space and keep the chosen parts of their bodies touching at all times, perhaps a hand on a knee, a heel on a leg.

● They need to try to keep their balance and keep their movements flowing.

● Ask which pairs of body parts are easiest to keep in contact? Which are hardest?

● Ask the pairs to line up in order from easy to difficult – easy to the left, difficult to the right, medium in the middle.

● Repeat the activity, each pair choosing a different pair of body parts.

## NOW TRY THIS

**1.** Ask them to start on the floor and gradually move to a standing position, all the time keeping contact with their partners. Remind them to keep changing positions.

**2.** Take photographs of stages of movement for display.

# TOOLED UP

**THINKING SKILL:** enquiry
**SUBJECT LINK:** design and technology
**LEARNING LINK:** visual
**ORGANISATION:** whole class
**RESOURCES:** a list of tools (with pictures if possible), for example, knife, ruler, scissors, hammer, saw, screwdriver, pliers, pencil, spanner

## WHAT TO DO

● Tell the children that it's very important to use tools carefully and safely.

● They are going to see how this is done.

● Ask for a volunteer.

● Ask them to mime using a tool.

● The children have to work out what the tool is and whether it's being used safely.

● The volunteer could then mime unsafe use so the children can see the difference.

● Now everyone has to mime using the tool. Encourage everyone to participate.

● Repeat with other tools, praising and drawing attention to safe use.

● Use this activity before any real use of tools.

# MOVE ALONG MATHS

**THINKING SKILL:** information processing
**SUBJECT LINK:** mathematics
**LEARNING LINK:** auditory, visual
**ORGANISATION:** two lines of children, facing each other
**RESOURCES:** a set of small cards with a range of simple questions related to your current mathematics focus (the answers written on the back) – enough for all children. Here are some sample questions:

---

*3 x 6*
*What is half of 22?*
*130 divided by 10*
*9 + 17*
*21 – 9*
*£10 shared equally by 4 people*
*Name any 4-sided shape (not a square)*
*How many cm in 2 metres?*
*How many mm in 2cm?*

---

## WHAT TO DO

- Split everyone into pairs ('A' and 'B'). All the 'A's sit in one line (a reasonable distance apart), and all the 'B's sit in a line facing their partner.
- If possible, the children sit along the edges of the room.
- Give each 'A' a different question card.
- 'A' reads their card to 'B' and holds it up for 'B' to read (not the answer).
- 'B' must answer the question quickly.
- When you clap your hands, 'A' flips the card round and shows 'B' the answer. The 'B's then have to move along to the next 'A' – the last 'B' 'falls off the end' and comes back to the beginning.
- Tell the children not to worry if they cannot answer the question or get it right – thinking about it is the important thing.
- How many questions can they answer in two minutes?
- Clap at appropriate times, based on the difficulty of the questions or the children's abilities.
- After two minutes, 'B's ask the questions and 'A's answer them. Use a new set of question cards.

# ROBOT DANCERS

**THINKING SKILL:** creative thinking
**SUBJECT LINK:** ICT
**LEARNING LINK:** auditory, visual
**ORGANISATION:** groups of four
**RESOURCES:** none required

## WHAT TO DO

- One person in your group is the controller and three are robots.
- The controller can make the robot do five things with these commands:
    *FORWARD _ STEPS – Walk forward _ steps*
    *LEFT – turn left a quarter turn*
    *RIGHT – turn right a quarter turn*
    *TWIST — wiggle bottom and move arms*
    *SHAKE – wobble arms and legs*
- Your challenge is to make up a robot dance of 15 commands (or less).
- Each robot must start and finish in the same place.
- Each robot must begin the dance within an arms reach of another robot.

# MOVE YOUR BODY

**THINKING SKILL:** information processing
**SUBJECT LINK:** design and technology
**LEARNING LINK:** visual, auditory
**ORGANISATION:** pairs
**RESOURCES:** a poster of a skeleton or a book with a diagram of a skeleton as a prompt for the children

## WHAT TO DO

- Decide who is 'A' and 'B'.
- 'A' will name a body part.
- 'B' must make a movement that uses that body part.
- For example, if 'A' says *knee bone*, 'B' could kneel or squat down.
- Take five turns each in naming and moving.

## NOW TRY THIS

Repeat but use the names of movements, for example, rotate, bend, grasp and so on.

# COMMUNITY SYMBOL

**THINKING SKILL:** evaluation
**SUBJECT LINK:** RE, PHSE
**LEARNING LINK:** visual
**ORGANISATION:** groups of four
**RESOURCES:** none required

## WHAT TO DO

● Explain that a community is a group of people who live or work together. Communities are great when people respect each other and get along, but not so good when people don't respect each other.

● Explain that the class is a community – of learners.

● Suggest finding a symbol to show that the class is a community.

● Ask them to use hands and arms to make a body symbol that means they all get along. Examples could be: hands and arms woven together, everyone shaking hands, fingers interlocked, arm-in-arm.

● Give examples and support as necessary.

● Each group demonstrates their body symbol.

● Ask them to decide which symbol was best and why.

● Hold a class vote.

# DANGEROUS WATER

**THINKING SKILL:** evaluation
**SUBJECT LINK:** mathematics
**LEARNING LINK:** visual
**ORGANISATION:** whole class
**RESOURCES:** a large open space; the numbers one to 40, each written on a piece of A4 card

## WHAT TO DO

● Spread the cards on the floor in the middle of the room, within stepping distance of each other.

● Gather the children to stand on one side of the cards, but don't step on them yet.

● Tell them that they are on the shore of a dangerous river. The only safe way to cross is by stepping on the numbers.

● 'Child-eating fraction-fish' (they fraction people before eating them) are swimming all around!

● There are many paths using the number stones across the river, but there are rules to follow to avoid the fraction fish.

● There has to be a connection between the number stones stepped upon – for example: only odd numbers or only numbers ending in zero or five.

● The children have to plan a route like this in their heads.

● Give them thinking time, then ask for volunteers.

● Watch as each child steps on the number cards – the class has to work out the connection between the numbers.

● Discuss what the connection was. Ask the crosser to share the pattern.

● Record the connection.

● Repeat as time allows, then ask which connection was the most interesting and why.

# PLANNING COUNCIL

**THINKING SKILL:** enquiry
**SUBJECT LINK:** geography
**LEARNING LINK:** visual, auditory
**ORGANISATION:** whole class
**RESOURCES:** a set of ideas related to geographical enquiry; a space for class to all stand up

*Sample ideas:*
*Knock down the swimming pool and build shops, restaurants and a play area in its place.*
*Plant more trees instead of building more houses.*
*Only allow buildings to be at the most three storeys high.*
*Build a lot more houses in the city.*
*Build a lot more houses in the country.*
*Plant trees and flowers along the motorways.*
*Divert rivers to bring them into the city.*
*(adapt these or create your own which can be related to the local area and/or previous work in geography)*

## WHAT TO DO

● You are members of a planning council who decide things like whether new buildings can be built or whether the landscape can be changed.

● Your teacher will read out a planning idea. Think about whether you agree with it.

● If you think it's a brilliant idea put your arms in the air and show ten fingers.

● If it's just OK, show five.

● If you don't agree, show no fingers.

● Find someone who had showed a different number of fingers. Talk about your different ideas for one minute.

# IN THE RIGHT PLACE AT THE RIGHT TIME

**THINKING SKILL:** enquiry
**SUBJECT LINK:** mathematics
**LEARNING LINK:** visual, auditory
**ORGANISATION:** whole class
**RESOURCES:** large working space; prompt sheet with questions such as:

*The product of 2 and 3 is…*
*The square root of nine is…*
*The sum of 5 and 3 is…*
*Double 3 is…*
*10 shared by 5 is...*
*4 halved is…*

## WHAT TO DO
● Find yourself a space and stand in it.
● Your teacher will read out the start of a maths sentence.
● You are going to finish the sentence by getting into a group that represents the answer.
● For example, if the sentence is *two multiplied by three is…* you need to get yourself into a group of six to show that six is the answer.
● If you cannot get yourself into a group, sit on the floor and wait for the next sentence.
● Your teacher will read out another sentence. Do the same thing again.
● Listen carefully as your teacher may use different words for the same operation. For example, *multiply* in one sentence and *product* in another.

# HOW DO YOU COMMUNICATE?

**THINKING SKILL:** evaluation
**SUBJECT LINK::** ICT
**LEARNING LINK:** visual, auditory
**ORGANISATION:** small groups
**RESOURCES:** a large working space; A4 paper and pencil for each group

## WHAT TO DO
● Ask the groups to record different ways that they communicate with people.
● Encourage a range of answers including non-verbal.
● Once they have recorded a range of methods, ask them to stop writing.

● Now they are going to act out some of these forms of communication.
● Each mini-performance must last exactly for a count of five.
● For example, they may be using the radio, email, or mobile phone.
● Each group has a turn at acting out one of their communication dramas, other children guessing what it is.

# SECRET TREASURE

**THINKING SKILL:** information processing
**SUBJECT LINK:** geography
**LEARNING LINK:** visual, auditory
**ORGANISATION:** pairs
**RESOURCES:** space to move between desk and viewing area (Captain's cabin); blank paper; pencils for each pair; copies of a simple island map, face down in viewing area (one map for each pair)

## WHAT TO DO
● Your challenge is to make a copy of the secret treasure map – there are only a limited number of copies. They must stay in the Captain's cabin.
● Watch out – when your teacher says *Captain's coming* you must put the map face down and return to your desk, so the Captain doesn't know you've been in his cabin.
● At your desk, start making a copy of the map from memory.
● When your teacher says *All clear*, your partner goes to the cabin to look at the map.
● When your partner hears *Captain's coming*, they return to your desk and you both add more to your own copy.
● Take it in turns to sneak into the cabin for a look – you will get five goes each lasting about 20 seconds.

# SCIENCE THEATRE

**THINKING SKILL:** creative thinking
**SUBJECT LINK:** science
**LEARNING LINK:** visual
**ORGANISATION:** groups of three
**RESOURCES:** none required

## WHAT TO DO

● You are going to use your bodies to be creative with science ideas.

● You've got two minutes to create a picture with your bodies inspired by one of the following phrases:

*A complete circuit*
*Solid, liquid, gas*
*Push and it'll push back*
*Help me grow!*
*The sun and the moon*
*Burning to ash*
*Dissolving away.*

● After two minutes, each group shows their work. The class guess which phrase is being illustrated.

# ELASTIC YES OR NO

**THINKING SKILL:** enquiry
**SUBJECT LINK:** PSHE
**LEARNING LINK:** auditory
**ORGANISATION:** whole class standing in a circle
**RESOURCES:** a large piece of elastic tied in a loop; closed questions related to PSHE work:

*Samples of closed questions:*
*If you commit a crime, does the law say you are responsible for it only if you're over 18?*
*Can people make other people feel happy?*
*Does it cost nearly £120,000 to bring up one child to the age of 18?*
*Is there a war anywhere in the world right now?*
*Is tolerance when you agree with other people?*
*Is it good for your health to eat fruit five times a year?*
*Can you legally open a bank account when you're seven?*

## WHAT TO DO

● Everyone holds the elastic with two hands and take a couple of steps backwards so that it stretches.

● Explain that you will ask some questions they

need to think about.

● They can answer *Yes* or *No*.

● If their answer is *Yes*, they let go with both hands and take a step back.

● If their answer is *No*, they keep hold and step forward.

● They should close their eyes so they can't see what anyone else does.

● Explain that they will have a count of five to think, then you will say *Answer* and they must hold on or let go straight away.

● Ask the first question, count down from five to one, and say *Answer*.

● They open their eyes – what has happened to the elastic?

● Discuss what the elastic says about the class answers. If it's on the floor: lots of yes answers and so on.

### ANSWERS

No, you are legally responsible if you are aged ten and over.
Yes, people can make other people happy.
Yes, it costs nearly £120,000 to bring up one child to the age of 18.
Yes, there are many wars taking place.
No, tolerance is respecting other people's ideas, but not changing your own.
No, you should eat fruit and vegetables five times a day.
Yes, you can open a bank account at the age of seven.

# AFFECTING EMOTION

**THINKING SKILL:** information processing
**SUBJECT LINK:** PSHE, RE
**LEARNING LINK:** visual
**ORGANISATION:** pairs
**RESOURCES:** pen and paper; a list of emotions on the board, for example: happy, sad, angry, scared, disgusted, surprised, confused

## WHAT TO DO

● Sit facing one another. One of you makes a face or strikes a pose to show one of the emotions written on the board, for example, a frown to show you're confused.

● Your partner has to identify the emotion and copy it.

● You then name one thing that gives you this emotion. For example, *I get confused if too many people speak to me at once.*

● Your partner now takes a turn.

● Work through as many emotions as you can.

# ALL CHANGE

**THINKING SKILL:** enquiry
**SUBJECT LINK:** PSHE, RE
**LEARNING LINK:** visual
**ORGANISATION:** whole class
**RESOURCES:** space for the class to sit together in a circle

## WHAT TO DO

● Ask the children to sit down in a circle making sure they can see everybody.
● Ask them to take a look around, notice who is where, what they are wearing, how they are sitting.
● Choose one child to leave the circle, close their eyes or leave the room.
● Explain that now they have left, you are going to make a change.
● Swap two people around, take someone's shoe off, swap shoes, remove someone's glasses, take a jumper off somebody.
● Once the change is made, the person outside can return. Can they spot the change?
● The person observing can ask two questions of the class.
● Once the change has been found, select another child to leave the circle. Make a different change.
● As they get better at spotting changes, make the changes more subtle.

# DIRECT ME TO THE COUNTER

**THINKING SKILL:** information processing
**SUBJECT LINK:** geography
**LEARNING LINK:** visual, auditory
**ORGANISATION:** pairs
**RESOURCES:** a compass for each pair or NSEW marked on the floor so everyone can see it; a counter for each pair; a large working space

## WHAT TO DO

● Decide who is 'A' and who is 'B'.
● Make sure you have a compass (or can see NSEW) and a counter.
● 'B' has to close their eyes while 'A' hides the counter somewhere in the working space.
● Once the counter is hidden, 'B' opens their eyes.
● 'A' must now direct 'B' to the counter using detailed information such as, *Take six steps*

*north. Turn to face east and then take three steps.*
● You can both use the compass to work out which way north is and for further directions.
● Once the counter is found, swap roles so that 'B' has a turn hiding the counter and 'A' has to find it.

# EXPLAINING A FEELING

**THINKING SKILL:** information processing
**SUBJECT LINK:** PSHE, RE
**LEARNING LINK:** visual, auditory
**ORGANISATION:** individual
**RESOURCES:** a large space, for example, a hall or playground; the following prompts written on the board:

---

*You see a friend on the other side of the road.*
*You are about to say your first line in the school play.*
*You have just found a pound coin on the floor.*
*You are lost on a crowded beach.*
*You are taking your pet to the vet.*
*It is your birthday.*
*Someone has stood on your toe – you don't think it was an accident!*

---

## WHAT TO DO

● Ask the children to walk slowly and carefully around the room, without bumping into anyone.
● When you read out a situation from the board, the children imagine how they would feel in that situation. They should show their feelings in their faces and how they walk or stand.
● When you say, *Freeze*, they must stand still.
● When you tap individuals on the shoulder, they must explain how they are feeling in that situation.
● The children have to listen carefully and prepare their feelings when you read out the next situation. They can start moving again when you say, *Action!*